The Art of Making Money

ISHMAIL HAMED

Copyright © 2019 Ishmail Hamed
All rights reserved
First Edition

PAGE PUBLISHING, INC.
New York, NY

First originally published by Page Publishing, Inc. 2019

ISBN 978-1-68456-943-4 (Paperback)
ISBN 978-1-68456-944-1 (Digital)

Printed in the United States of America

Contents

Author's Note 5

Part 1: The Millionaire's Mind Technology Process

- Introduction - 9
- *Chapter 1:* The Road Ahead 19
- *Chapter 2:* Magazine Dreams! 28
- *Chapter 3:* Platinum Plans! 41
- *Chapter 4:* Get Your Mind Right! 62

Part 2: From Point A to Point Money!

- *Chapter 5:* Boss Mode 79
- *Chapter 6:* Build Winning Business Blueprints 90
- *Chapter 7:* Finance Your Business Operation 111
- *Chapter 8:* Building Your First Business 125
- *Chapter 9:* - Manage Your Profit Portfolio 138
- *Chapter 10:* Evolve Your Platinum Plan 152

Afterword 165
Notes 167

Author's Note

Welcome to *The Art of Making Money*! This is the **hottest** book on the **market** for **making money** today! When I recently looked at the state of our **American** economy and all the tragic effects of **Brexit**, I was moved to write a book to help people regain **financially** what they had lost. Call it my humble offering. When I finally took on the **challenge** of writing this book, I knew that there was currently a **plethora** of books on the **market** for making **money** today. Upon realizing how many books were out there, I made a **promise** to myself that if I were to write this book that it would have to deliver and really show **you** a realistic way to make some real **money**. So at that time, I cleared off my desk and then cleared my **mind** of anything that would bear a resemblance to any of the other books available on the **market** and began to sketch the outline for this **book**.

What separates this book from the rest is that this book is not **conceived** through the practice of **crystal ball gazing** and **reading tea leaves** to make **financial prophecies**. These are ugly practices that many authors have surrendered to today when offering us what they **believe** to be valuable **financial information**. These books and their ideas have become a great hindrance for all of us across America and the world who are currently seeking to discover **solid financial information**. So the greatest challenge when writing this book was to write a **logical book** that could guide you from **point A to point money**! And after an excruciating amount of **research, time, energy,** and **hard work,** I can now truly say *eureka*! **Mission accomplished**! Follow me now through the pages of this book and let me show you *The Art of Making Money*! **Let's Go!**

Part 1

The Millionaire's Mind Technology Process

- The Art of Making Money -

- Introduction -

    We all want to know the *secrets* of life such as how to become **rich** and *famous*. We want **first-class information** explaining how we can make some **money** right now **today** if not **yesterday**! The *new world* of the **twenty-first century** that we live in allows for us to *locate* whatever **financial information** that our minds can possibly *conceive* of by *logging* on to the **Internet** and **Googling** away. The **Internet** literally places the world at our fingertips. With all this **information** available to us, much of the good stuff, like how to really make some big money is usually buried away deep in the minds of the **rich** and **famous**. And who would want to reveal their *secrets* anyway, huh? Well, never fret because with my *new* **millionaires mind technology** book, ***The Art of Making Money***, I kick in the door wide open where you can now have access to all the **valuable information** that you will need on your **money-motivated mission!**

    The **millionaires mind technology** is **designed** for the *new age* **entrepreneurs** of the **future**. At present, we live in a *new world* of the *future* where the *technologically advanced* future of our **dreams** has begun to take shape! **Today is not like yesterday!**

    Today we have big **dreams** of **rising up, shining hard, and accumulating money** in **large amounts**! Today we desire success that at least does not take a lifetime to **achieve**. With this being our state, it is necessary that we **discover new paths** for *achieving* the **American dream** and more *creative ways* to **achieve** what generations past could not.

    Today across **America**, we are desperate for *new solutions* to help put some real money in our pockets as swiftly as possible. With

America's economy, Europe's economy as well as other *economies* across the **globe** that have a *direct effect* upon our *pockets* in the worst possible conditions that the world has seen in many moons. We are losing confidence in every *market economy* that has given us comfort and *peace of mind* in the past. We **see** our *hard-earned money* being *thrown away* through faulty decision-making in the hallways of the *White House* and the *corporate offices* of *big business*. And now, *we have become painfully aware that if we are to lift ourselves up from where we are today financially to where we desire to be that we must move in a new direction*! We must jump in the driver's seat and take the wheel rather than continue to go along for the ride. The only **problem** is how. This book is *designed* to *solve* this **problem**.

In this book, **The Art of Making Money**, I will lay it all out for you and put in plain words a **program** that will help show you **how to** create your own personal **million**-dollar **platinum plan** for what I call making your **magazine dream** come true to life! The **magazine dream** is the **new American dream**! It is the **universal dream** that many **Americans** *share* today of becoming **rich, powerful**, and **famous**. Where basically in your life you **rise up, shine hard,** and **accumulate riches** in **large amounts**! The **magazine dream** is a dream that can **splash** your **face** across the cover of popular magazines such as **People, Time, Vogue, Oprah's O Magazine, Ebony, Essence, Cosmopolitan, Forbes,** or **Fortune**. We hold this **dream** today because we live in a **fast-paced, high-tech** world where we **see** people becoming **millionaires** in **record numbers**! And *we want* in on all the **big money** that we see *flowing around us*!

It seems that every time that we turn on our **televisions**, or log on to the ***Internet*** that we see people going from *rags to riches* overnight in the **music business** in almost every genre of *popular music* that we *Americans* enjoy! Then we see **Hollywood** manufacturing *stars* and fattening their bank accounts beyond reason! **America's top models** are prancing around, strutting their stuff on the catwalks, and rising to **fortune** and **fame**. Then the world of **professional sports** is another popular **path** that people are taking to *rise to* *riches* in our day. Seeing these constant stories of **rags to riches**, we quickly develop a **hunger** for our own *piece of the pie*. The **desire** to get rich is *aroused* within us, and we want in! The siren call to riches becomes *irresistible* because the **glamorous lifestyle** that we see the *stars* are living is *very attractive*, *highly seductive*, and *extremely* hard to ignore! Seeing all this **big money** being made makes us want to get some of this **big money** for ourselves so that we can live like our favorite stars do.

But for the people across **America** who work for a living, becoming a **millionaire** in this lifetime seems so unrealistic because a silent *subliminal message* is sent to our minds that reads if you want to become *rich* and *famous* in **America**, you either must *rap*, *sing*, *dance*, be born as *beautiful* as a *model*, or have a *special talent* that allows for you to excel in the world of *sports*. So the *problem* it seems is that if you don't *rap, sing, dance, model, or play professional sports* in **America** that you are doomed to sit on the sidelines and watch this *beautiful* **American dream** life pass you by. So I have written this book specifically for those people who do not *rap, sing, dance, model,* or *play professional sports* but still *desire* to **make big money**! There are so many **paths** to **making millions** in this world. But every **path** is not for everybody. So you must find your own **path**.

So to win in this **new world**, you will have to be *open-minded, psychologically flexible,* and *able to adapt.* This book will help *guide* you on how you can begin transforming your *thinking* so that you can begin to see **America** and the world through **new eyes**.

New eyes that will allow you to see the *quickest*, most *effective* way to **make your first million** dollars! Seeing **America** and the world through **new eyes** is the *process* of *shifting* your *thinking* to develop within your mind a **money-conscious** and **business mind**. Through this mind-*shifting* process, you can begin the process of *transforming* your life from **rags to riches**. With **new eyes**, you can *focus* to begin the *process* of studying your life and the world to *intelli-*

gently **see** the many **models** of *American* **success**. And with an **eye** looking to uncover the perfect **path** that you can possibly follow to *climb to the top*. In this book, I will articulate a **model** of *American* **success** that you can *duplicate* and *clone* for yourself as *a pattern for your rise*.

You must begin to *shift* your *thinking*. *Why?* Because as I have stated, the world that we now live in shapes our perceptions to *believe* that if we are to *achieve* our **dreams** of **riches** and becoming a **millionaire** that we must follow one of the paths that we **see** on **television**, or on the ***Internet***. This is very important. Why? The reality is that the odds and chances of *achieving riches* in the *music business*, or in *Hollywood*, *professional sports* or becoming the world's *next top model* are astronomical and would be similar to winning the *mega millions* playing the **lottery**. The truth is every day, **Americans** need more *realistic, practical* **paths** that we can follow for *accumulating big money*! The question then now is how do you realistically **make your first million** if you do not have some extraordinary *gift* that you can offer the world in exchange for ***riches***?

Answering this question becomes so confusing because there are so many **paths** in ***America*** and the world that you can possibly follow to ***rise to riches***. And even if someone has followed a specific **path** that has led to their own **individual success**, the fact remains that you and I must find our own **path** to **success** in life. Just as two identical twins born from the same mother, birthed from the same womb shall still have to live their own individual unique lives and find their own way. So the same principle applies to our **ambitions** to *gain wealth* in the world. With your life's own set of unique *financial circumstances* facing you today to answer the question you must *intelligently* and *insightfully zoom* your *mind's eye* in to **study** your world to uncover a **path** that you can take to **climb the ladder** of *success*. And after my research of ***America*** and the world, I have come to *believe* and am completely convinced that the quickest, most *effective* **path** for you to take to **make your first million** is through the doorway of your *dreams*!

So now if you are to embark on your **money-motivated mission**, then you must start **dreaming big**! As I researched the *American* money game, I learned that the *quickest*, most *effective* way for **making** a **million** dollars in **America's** *new economy* is to enter the world of **entrepreneurship**. Through the doorway of **entrepreneurship**, you can enter the **game** and begin investing in **business opportunities** that can possibly make you **millions** of dollars! To win in the **money game** you will first need to acquire the precise tools to start building your *house of success*! The *millionaires mind technology* program that you have here is the specific tools that you will need to *succeed*! Here I will clearly instruct you on how you can find your own **path** *step-by-step*. This is a course of action that many have followed to **achieve millionaire** status. It is a **model** of *success*!

Now to begin the *millionaires mind technology* process of upgrading your perspective, you will first need to examine your past. This is **key**. Start *rewinding your mind back in time* to the tender days of your childhood when you were *young* and *impressionable*. You must start the process at this point in your mind. Why? Because it is a fact that when we are young, it is usually at this point in our lives that our *perceptions* and **concepts** about *money* and how to *accumulate money* are usually *molded* and *shaped*. This childhood *programming period* then serves as the **foundation** of our *thought processes that we carry around with us in the world* today. It is this **programming** that causes us to *rise* or *fall financially*. If what we are taught about *money* and how to *accumulate money* in our *childhood* is flawed then most likely this *thinking* will lead us to *financial ruin* later on in life. For **proof** of this **fact**, just look at your **financial situation** right now **today**.

Now *zoom* your mind in to **imagine** what it is specifically that you were taught from your family, from your school, and other influential people that taught you about **money** and how to **make** some. For instance, in many of our schools across *America*, the question is traditionally asked, "**What do you want to become when you grow up, boys and girls?**" This question is *designed* to *stimulate* our *imaginations* and to *encourage* us to **dream**. Depending on our social backgrounds and our upbringing, we, as children, usually will answer this question with a safe, *run-of-the-mill*, *cookie-cutter* answer that fits the mold. We say things like I want to be a **doctor**, a **police officer**, a *fireman*, or a *lawyer*. And these are nice, safe **dreams**. But when children shoot past the mark with *bigger* **dream** choices, the children at that time are usually met with ridicule, scorn, and disapproval. This reaction creates *fear*, *anxiety*, and *confusion* if our **dreams** are **bigger**.

In schools as children, we are being taught to **dream** in a way that fits the mold of what society **believes** to be *realistic* **dreams** for children. This **dream-***shaping process* is where the **financial problems** that we develop in our lives usually begin. Our **financial problems** begin with our **thinking**. Following this line of **thought**, we are further **programmed** to **believe** that if we are not *lucky* enough to be born **rich** that **the road to success** in our lives is to *follow the* **path** *of going to school* and *getting good grades*. So we can go to a **swanky college** that will *provide* us with a **credential** that we can *offer* an *employer* for a good job. Then we are taught to ***visualize*** that *distant moment* in the future where we are *rewarded* with a **fat paycheck** and an even fatter **retirement plan** mixed with some other *attractive* **benefits**. Basically we are encouraged from a *young age* to develop ourselves into a **marketable product** that has a **strong market** value in the **job market**. This is what we are taught. But as we follow this **path**, that *distant moment* in the future that has been **programmed** into our minds never actually seems to ***materialize***.

Following this **path** in life, we get stuck living **check to check**. Stuck *running* on a **financial** *hamster wheel*. So it is safe to say that a college degree doesn't promise us a thing. Because if you look, you will **see** that there are people across **America** with college degrees that are being forced to work labor jobs to pay the bills. And with this reality, we **see** flaws in the way we are **programmed** to *think* as children. So these days, if you **plan** to make some big money, *change* your **thinking**! And set your sites on *new creative* ways to **generate income**. Understanding **business ownership** is the **solution**! Why? Because as children, we are taught to **dream** of becoming an *employee* rather than to **dream** of becoming the **boss**! So is it **clear** to see how this **dream** choice holds us back in life!

Okay, so take the time-out right now to stop and *think* about who really stands to gain the biggest piles of **money** the fastest between the **bosses** of our world and the **employees**.

Think! If every morning *millions* of people in cities across *America* wake up, get dressed, and then head off to a job working in an office, a retail location, or maybe a warehouse in the **role** of an **employee** while at the same exact time, there are other people who wake up each morning headed to the same locations to play the role as *business owner* and *boss*. It should be obvious then to notice that if the *businesses owners* are the ones creating all the **jobs** that we are trained to go out into the world and get and writing all the paychecks, then the *business owner bosses* are the ones making all the **big money** in the world, right? So to financially break free of this subservient role and to begin moving in a new direction in your life where you follow a **path** that will allow you a faster, more realistic, practical approach for accumulating some big money, then you must *shift* your *thinking* in the direction of adopting **entrepreneurship** as your **career path**.

Know that **business ownership** is the *future* of **America** and the world. Why? With the dream of **business ownership**, you can rise as high as your *talents* and *intelligence* will allow you to go in life! While with the employment **dream,** you can only rise as high as your **boss** will allow. So in this book, I will introduce you to the world of **entrepreneurship** to help you step into the role of **business owner** rather than the **role** of **employee**. Here you will be exposed to how to start **thinking** like a boss and *how-to* develop a **platinum plan** around *investing* in **business** ideas that can potentially help you to make your **first million**. So **entrepreneurship** is the **path** and **model of success** that you must follow to reach the *highest heights* of *financial achievement* in *America* today!

It is a fact that many of the *greatest* **big-money success** *stories* in **Americans**, *past* and *present*, are stories of *great* **American entrepreneurs**! For case in point, **Bill Gates** and **Warren Buffett**, ranked as two of the *richest people in the world*, are simply *brilliant* **business owners**. To further illustrate, **Oprah Winfrey, Mark Zuckerberg, Mark Cuban**, and **Donald Trump** are all **successful American entrepreneurs**. Jay-Z, Sean *"P. Diddy"* **Combs, Dr. Dre**, and **Russell Simmons** are **great examples** of *successful* **American entrepreneurs** in the **business arena**. The choice of **business ownership** opens to you an **aggressive investment vehicle** that offers you **more options, more control** over **your life, more control** over your **financial future**, and ultimately, **more control** over your *destiny*. **Business ownership** opens to you more avenues to **achieve** your **short-term** as well as your **long-term financial goals**. It is a **solid investment vehicle** that can **potentially** give you a greater **return** on **your investment!**

Imagine that when you enter the **job market** that you are *choosing* an **automobile** as your **vehicle** for **reaching** your **dreams**. Then *imagine* that when you *choose* **entrepreneurship** as your vehicle for *achieving* your **dreams** that you are *choosing* an **airplane**! Competitively **comparing** the **advantages** of *flying* compared to *driving* when you are *traveling closer* to your **dreams**, it is **obvious** that with an **airplane** as your vehicle, you can rise higher and move toward your dreams faster once you get moving *down the runway* and *then take flight*! So adopting **entrepreneurship** as your career path greatly enhances your chances of making your life a success! Following the career **path** of **entrepreneurship** can *change* one's **financial** *fortune* through the process of *creating* **new businesses** around **new markets** that are on the **rise!**

Now *imagine* that everything *in the universe moves* in **cycles**. Such as daily, the **sun** and the **moon** are **moving** in a **cycle**. And yearly, the **summer, winter, spring**, and **fall** are **moving** in seasonal **cycles**. The same sorts of **cycles** *exist* in the **game** of **money** in **America**. So **believe** that whatever the **financial weather** that exist today, the

cycles of our economy will continue to present *opportunities* to make **millions** for **entrepreneurs** with **platinum plans** for making their **magazine dreams** come true! It is the *new* **millennial generation** of **money-conscious, business-minded Americans** that will **lift us up** to new *higher heights* of **achievement** here in **America**! Like the *original generations* of **Americans** who established this nation acting on their **bold ideas**, you must step up to the plate and become one of the next generations of **star entrepreneurs** to do **big things**! The **American business arena** is where the **big action** is today!

Following this **path**, the first generations of **Americans** embodied the **entrepreneurial** *spirit*. Their **ambition, drive**, and **deep determination** to **win** was born from a deep sense of manifest *destiny*. And this concept of **manifest destiny** is born from the **dream**! The great **American dream** of living the **good life**, getting **filthy rich**, and living like a **fat cat**! And what is wrong with that? So now you must put on your *thinking* cap so that you can begin your **money-motivated mission**! But before we move forward, I must say this. As with anything in life, nothing is ever guaranteed. So know that the results that you gain from this book, *The Art of Making Money*, will absolutely be based upon how **effectively** you can absorb the **information** in this book, then how well you can take the **information** out of this book and put it in *motion* in your life. The fact that you have this book in your hands is an admirable sign that you are **ready** to take the leap.

I am **putting** these *thoughts* on your *mind* **straight** out of the **gate** just as a **warning** so that you will **not** be **misled** to **believe** that transforming your financial reality will be a **cake walk**. Rather, it will be quite the contrary. We know that everything in this life that has any real value never comes easy! Think. For anyone to **make their first** *million* will be a **struggle** and a *real* **challenge**. So know that your **financial success** will depend a great deal upon the **type** of person that you are and the way that you are **built**.

Accumulating **your first *million*** will require that you develop *gold-medal focus* in *the environment* of your **mind**. It will take **ambition, deep drive, determination,** and **heavy motivation** and **sky hustle**. I will help you develop a ***clear vision*** of your **platinum plans goals** and hopefully stir within you a **burning desire** to **get rich in your soul** so that your **Magazine dreams** will become an **inevitable reality**.

But you must develop an **unshakable drive** and **determination** to follow your **dreams** topped with an iron will to see your dreams through, then it is there that you can possibly begin living the ***new* American magazine dream** in your life! As an aspiring star player in the ***American* money game** understands that it does not matter if you have *limited education, limited resources,* or *technical know-how.* In the ***American* money game,** know that you can win if you have the **courage** to try! **America** is the land of **vast opportunity** where *big* **dreams come true**! This is your **new path** to **success** that has now **opened up** to you! So now if you are **ready** to take flight on your **money-motivated mission**, then fasten your seatbelt, prepare for lift off, and **let's go**!

ISHMAIL

Chapter 1

The Road Ahead

Now let's look to **the road ahead**. It is **believed** that if you are to **know** where you are **headed** in the *future*, you first must take a look **back** into the **past**. But *looking* back into our *history* could have never *prepared* us for the **financial storm** that we are in the midst of today. **Today is not like yesterday.** Today we live in a *new world* and are in a new place **financially**! Today times have *drastically* changed from what we have come to know about our **money** and **finances** yesterday. With the **new world** *financial* conditions that have *taken shape*, if you are to ***survive***, you must **strive** to gain full *control* over your **finances,** which ultimately allows you to **gain control** over your **life**! It is taking your **financial destiny** into your own hands that will lead to your **financial freedom**!

To begin the ***process*** of **making your first million**, you must know that everything will start with you developing the *proper perceptions* in your **mind**. So initially through the ***millionaires mind technology*** *process*, I will *suggest* first that you do some **research** aimed at developing an *accurate perception* in your **mind** of the *financial* **world**, your **personal finances** and then begin to *imagine* in what *direction* you would like to go **money wise**. To move in a *new direction* in your **financial life**, you will need to start making some **critical decisions**. You must **decide** that you are **ready** and **willing** to do whatever it takes to **make it happen**! Why? Your **financial circumstances** will only **change** when you **decide** to *create* a well-*thought*-out **plan** to change your **path**.

It is through the *process* of making this **decision** that will open to you the *possibilities* of you gaining your full share of **material wealth** in this world and *rising* to **achieve** your *desired* **level** of success! *Understanding* and *applying* this **millionaires mind technology** *principle* will be key to you **making your first million**. Why? Know that in the **money game** you can only have **money** in the **amounts** that you **strive** for! If you only **strive** for a **small paycheck**, then you can't expect to hustle up a million bucks. To **win**, you must no longer be content with the *illusion* of *financial stability* that a **paycheck** has to offer you. Rather to **make your first million**, you must begin **striving** to be **made** out of **money**, rolling in the **dough, affluent, wealthy, loaded,** and with **money** to **blow**. To accomplish this, you will need to locate **new reliable sources** of **income**. So get it in your head right now that **entrepreneurship** is the *smartest* **career path** in our **new economy** that can **provide** you with **new reliable sources** of **income!**

Business ownership is the *future*. Let's take a look at why this is so true. In recent years, a *few major events* in **America** and across the world have had a **heavy impact** upon our *finances*. To *discover* where we are headed in the *future*, I will *suggest* that you turn your **attention** to current *news broadcast* that *flash* around the world daily on our **televisions** and the ***Internet***. Begin by *looking* at the *news stories* with a *skilled* **eye** to *intelligently analyze* what it is we are *seeing* and *hearing*. The **news headlines** jump out at us with *stories* filed with widespread panic among **Americans** do to the *destabilization* of our **economy** and **mass job loss**. We are hearing of many hardworking **Americans** who suddenly are watching their *nest egg savings rapidly* evaporate into thin air after years of ***believing*** that their **money** was safe. And this only seems to be the **beginning**.

The hardest hit among us are the hardworking ***Americans*** who have *invested* many valuable years of their lives in the *job market* only to have *their personal stock value plummet* and lose everything. Another hard hit group in our society is the newly **graduated college students** who recently entered the work force in the aftermath of our **great recession**. These two groups are finding themselves in a fierce competition for the few jobs that are available in the ***job market***. And even for the people who are fortunate enough to already have a good job today, there still is actually no such thing as **job security**. So it is clear to *see* that *regardless of where people are starting from*, or where they have been in the **job market**, the fact of the matter is that *all around the board* for now and into the foreseeable *future*, it seems that *good jobs* will be hard to come by.

Further, the *national unemployment* rate is *forecasted* to remain as high as **8.5 percent** for many years into the *future*. Why? The aftershock caused from a **great recession** can **echo** for years. **A recession that ends today can take up to ten to twenty years from now to fully recover the loss of damages that have been inflicted upon our finances.** So you see that things will not change anytime soon in the *job market*. So now ask yourself. Can you possibly afford to continue following this *path* if it leads to nowhere? Following the *path* of a typical **nine**-to-**five** today only promises *headaches*. While following the path of **entrepreneurship** that I have described allows for you to broaden the *scope* of your **financial ambitions** and *opens* the door through which your **million-dollar dreams** can *soar*! This is the *future* of **America,** and like it or not, the *future* is here now! It is *out* with the old and in with the *new*! Instead of *following* the old *path* of looking for a **job**, today you have to **adapt** to these *new times*, get **smart,** and **create** your own **dream job**!

Creating a **business** that you *own* and *control* in essence **creates** your very own **dream job** where you don't ever have to worry about being **fired** or **downsized**. Why? Because you will be the **boss**! So the **million-dollar question** for you to ask yourself is "**Would** you rather be **safe** with a regular **nine-to-five job,** or would you rather **start your own business** and **become** the **boss**?" And what is *safety* in today's **job market** anyway? The only real *safety* that you will find today is **investing** in yourself. In this situation, the saying "**The bigger the risk, the bigger the rewards**" is very true. But do not mistake what I'm saying to mean that you should take a blind leap. Not at all! You must take *careful, calculated steps* that will allow for you to *maximize the probability of your success*. To win, you must follow this *new path forward* to secure your ***financial future***. You must **believe** and take a leap of **faith**! At this point in time, you are at a *defining moment* in your life where you must *decide* whether you will take the leap and burst forward on a bold *new path* of **entrepreneurship,** or you will be content with a typical **nine-to-five** job?

If you are seeking a *new path forward* in your life for **making your first million,** then it is all systems go and you will now begin your *journey* into the world of **business ownership**! If you are still undecided, then maybe you should just put this book down now! *My friend, if I could cause a bolt of lightning to descend from the sky at this very moment to strike you and electrify your soul causing you to suddenly experience a moment of clarity opening your eyes to realize the major opportunity that has been laid out here in America before any go-getter with a platinum plan for making a million dollars, then I would*! But I cannot, so you must come to *realize* this fact for yourself and discover creative ways to **capitalize** on the *economic conditions* that have arrived.

Turbulent conditions have arrived. But the cycles of our *economy* whether we are in a boom or bust cycle will continue to provide **opportunities** for you to **make your first million**! And now more than ever, the time is ripe for you to enter the **business arena.** Why? Because with all of the stories of doom and gloom that we *hear* about in the *media* remember that we are still living in **America,** the land of *unimaginable progress* and *barrier-breaking prosperity*! For any **money-conscious, business-minded** individual skillfully looking at the *big picture,* it is easy to observe that behind all of the world market *financial volatility,* a **new economic order** is being ushered in and that we are at the dawn of another *major economic upswing.* If you are **business savvy,** you will recognize that the negative *economic conditions* that have *formed* across the nation has actually opened the door up to the possibly the most *opportune moment* in history of **America** to accumulate a fortune since the conception of the *thirteen colonies.*

So from this point forward, I will propose that you use **entrepreneurship** as your vehicle for **making your first million dollars**!

Entering the **business arena** will allow you access a *new world* where you can *re-create yourself, restructure your finances,* and *reset* your **income**! The **business arena** is the world of **buying** and **trading** things among people for a **profit**. All across **America,** there is **money** here for the taking in the **business arena** if you know what to look for! In this **arena,** there are almost limitless **opportunities** to make a **million** bucks! **Business** drives our world. Behind any of the *greatest fortunes* that have been made in **America** is a lucrative **business**. In **America,** with one **hot business concept** and a **platinum plan,** you can possibly be lifted to higher heights of **success** in due time. But you have got to be in the **money game** to **win** it!

Every **rap star, rock star, super model,** or **movie star** needs a stage to perform and shine on just as every **professional athlete** requires a *playing field* that fits their **talents** and **skills** to *do their thing on*. When you **step** into the **shadow** of the **entrepreneur,** the world will become *your stage to shine on*! Now as I have previously **declared** and will continue to shout until it sticks in your **brain**, it all starts with you turning your *vision* to begin *looking* at the world through **new eyes**! **New eyes** that can see the **vast** *opportunity* that **America** offers you to **rise** in the **business arena**. In the **business arena,** you can *rise* as high as your **talents** and **intelligence** will allow you to go! You have everything laid out in front of you in the **American free market system** to **get rich**! Across **America** from **city** to **city** in the **business arena,** there is always **money** and **opportunity ready** and **willing** to respond to anyone **bold** enough to go out and **get it!**

Now **picture this**: Many people will live average lives filled with poverty and lack not because they were **destined** to fail. They live this way because they never actually *opened* their **eyes** to **see** all of the **money** and **opportunity** *surrounding* them. Open your *eyes* now to **see** that **building businesses** to *compete* in the **American business arena** can offer you the **opportunity** to **get rich** that you *seek*. That is, if you **harness** the **power** that **exist** within it. It is in this **arena** where you can find the **opportunity** to **make your first million** dollars! **Think**. If competing in the **American business arena** has helped people like **Steve Jobs**, **Mark Zuckerberg**, **Donald Trump**, **Warren Buffett**, **Oprah Winfrey**, **Jay-Z**, **Bill Gates**, **Sean Combs**, and **Martha Stewart** accumulate **millions** and **billions** of dollars. Then it is in this **arena** that you can shine and do your thing! So it's clear that you must follow the path of **entrepreneurship** to make it happen!

I have heard it said that in *America* today, that there is a serious lack of **money** and **opportunity** because foreigners are coming in and stealing them from right up under our noses. Now ask yourself. Why is it that this could take place if this argument is true? It is true because they have *eyes* to *see* the vast **money** and **opportunity** that can be gained through **building businesses** in **America**. We take it for granted while the foreigners are smart enough to come in and *capitalize* on the *opportunities* by setting up **businesses** in our cities across **America**. This is *money* flowing through **America** that you yourself can begin to compete for and get if you do the same thing. All you have to do is put on your **go-getter goggles** and get in the **money game**! If you *open up your eyes,* you will *see* in cities across **America** that there are many new **markets** on the *rise*! New **markets** that are giving birth to **products** that you can offer to sell to the consuming public that has a *strong* **demand**. In your city, you can begin to *attract* some of this **money** from your community's purses and wallets into your pockets by **building** *new* **businesses**.

Building a **business** around a *new* **market trend** born from a **strong demand** can *become a gold mine that you can exploit.* Your **business**, if **built** around a *new* **product** that is in **demand**, can *blossom* and *grow* into a **money-making machine**! Hot *new* **products** that are in **demand** are born from people's **desires, wants, needs,** and pressing **problems**. Uncovering people's **desires, wants, needs,** and **problems** will be the *key* to your **success**! Any of these **four elements**, if discovered, are the **ingredients** for **making your first million** bucks! **Example**: all of the **economic evils** that we are seeing in the media today can be a *subliminal signal* that there is no better day than today to go into **business** for yourself! **Think** of the **strong demand** that these conditions have created!

Business concept: **America's** failing economy has created widespread **problems** that millions of people across **America** share. **America's** failing economy then presents a **major opportunity** to make **millions**! How? People are desperately looking for **solutions**. These **problems** are a major **opportunity** to **make millions** if you can discover creative ways to *develop* **products** around solving these **widespread problems** that we face. **Think. Demand** in **business** equals **profits**. People **demand** *solutions* today because people are **losing their jobs, losing their savings, losing their homes,** and things are falling apart. So as an **entrepreneur,** notice that where people are losing everything, there is **money** to be made! The suggestion is that in the midst of great tragedy, a tremendous *opportunity* to *make millions* is presented to you if you are a **business-minded** individual with a **platinum plan** for **making your first million**!

Starting up a **new business** right now could possibly be the best **decision** that you ever made. Your **product,** if properly *designed,* can possibly make you **millions** *capitalizing* off this ***new*** hot **market** that has *opened up* due to our economy. As I have stated, ***new*** hot **products** developed around the vast sea of **pressing problems** that **America** and the world face right now and will continue to face for many years into the *future* can provide you with the **opportunity** to make **millions** that you *seek*! Understanding this, it should *become clear* for you **see** that if you develop the *proper perception* of things **financial** that there may be a vast range of *money-making opportunities* surrounding you at this very moment! You, as an **entrepreneur,** must uncover any one of people's **desires, wants,** needs, or **pressing problems** that may exist and find a creative way to *capitalize* from these *by creating* **products** *that* **match** *and* **satisfy** *the* **need** *that you* **uncover.**

So whether you **dream** of becoming a *millionaire* or even a *billionaire,* you must begin your journey through first recognizing that climbing the *ladder of success* in the **American business arena** will be a **process**. This **process** will consist of you **building your first business** and then **making your first million** bucks dollar for dollar. *As you hustle every dollar that reaches your hands from any business-generating activities will move you a step closer to your million-dollar goal. While every dollar that you spend aimlessly moves you a step back.* Through this **process** of you learning **how to make your first million**, you will first have to *learn how to make a hundred thousand; and to make hundred thousand, you must first learn ways to make some thousands; and to make some thousands, you will have to learn ways to hustle up some hundreds; and to make some hundreds, you will need a few green dollars to invest. Getting your hands on a lump sum of money that you can invest in your first business may possibly be one of the biggest challenges that you face. But if you are determined, you will do what it takes to win!*

My friend, sometimes life leads us to a defining moment where our life's circumstances will force us to **open** up our **eyes**. Our **eyes** are **opened** up where we begin to **see** *new* doors to a bigger, brighter future **opening** up. And when that door **opens** up at that time, it offers you a **choice**. This **choice** is a **choice** that must be made alone. At that time, you may **choose** to move forward in a *new direction* in your life, or you can **choose** to keep following the **path** that you have followed in your life thus far. So today, you yourself must make a **decision**. You must **decide** whether you will follow the **program** that I have laid out for you in this book that is designed to lead you toward a bigger, brighter future in your life, or whether you will continue on the *path* that you are on today.

If you are to go the distance, then first you must embrace the **entrepreneurial** *spirit*. The **American entrepreneurial** *spirit* is what has made **America** great! The **American entrepreneur** is the *ultimate* **prototype** or **model** of **American success**! The **American entrepreneur** is an **innovator** of **business enterprise** who sees **money-making opportunities** where others don't. The **American entrepreneur** organizes **business operations** to exploit these **business opportunities** for **financial gain** by assembling the necessary factors of **production** to **supply** a **demand. This is where the money is at.** To make a **million,** you will need to **invest** in any of the many **business opportunities** that **entrepreneurial** talents **invest** in across **America.** Now you must get into the **money game** and begin **investing** in **business opportunities** that will allow you to begin:

- Generating a solid **stream** or **streams** of **income**!

- Turning some **profits**!

- Fattening your **pockets** and **bank accounts**!

- And stacking up some **green dollars** to **make your first million**!

Note: From the point that you **decide** to get into the **money game**, each day of your life should be spent discovering **new creative** ways to turn a buck. Understand that you do not make a **million** dollars in one lump even though it is possible. The **process** is to **hustle, stack, save,** then **reinvest** to **expand** and **grow**. Accumulate **money** each day to gradually move toward your **million-**dollar **goal.** You must use each day of your life strategically as a stepping stone to progress and move closer to your **Dreams. Let's go!**

Chapter 2

Magazine Dreams!

A journey of a thousand miles begins with the first step. Your **million-**dollar journey will begin with your *dreams*! ***America*** is the land where big *dreams* come true! So you are in luck since **America's** conception of people have been drawn from every corner of the earth to come live the *American dream*! And now today, there is a *new* **American dream** called the **magazine dream**! The **magazine dream** is the **dream** of rising up, shining hard, and accumulating **money** in large amounts! It is a **dream** that can splash your face across popular **magazine** such as **Fortune** and **Forbes** *magazines*. The **magazine dream** is a **dream** of having **money** to buy **luxury cars, big jewelry, designer-label clothing, mansions, yachts, private jets, extravagant vacations, exquisite food,** and **basically** the **best** the world has to offer you! The **magazine dream** is you living your own version of a modern-day **manifest destiny**!

Your very own version of a modern-day **manifest destiny** is where you are *surrounded* by the *finest things* that this life has to offer. You will be born through your **magazine dream**s! Now to begin the *millionaires mind technology* **process,** you will need to perform some psychological exercises, which I call **money meditations.** Performing a **money meditation** is the **process** of you **developing** and **defining** your **dreams** in your **mind.** The **goal** with the **money-meditation process** is to help you to begin developing a mental **blueprint** from which you can sketch out your **million-**dollar *platinum plan*!

The **money-meditation process** is the first **fundamental step** in the *millionaires mind technology* process. The **money meditations** will help to *set in motion* the *process* of you **upgrading** your **perspective, remixing** your *outlook* of the **future,** and developing in your *mind* an **unambiguous vision** of the **road ahead** that you will follow. Understand your *rise* to **success** will begin **within** your mind. So the **process** of *re***programming** your *mind* for **success** will begin with **transforming** your **thinking**. The **transformation** of your **thinking** will open up a *new* doorway. Through the **money-mediation process,** you will begin *shifting* your **thinking** to **rethink** what is *possible* in your life. It is through this **process** that you will develop a **mental blueprint**. This **process** will help you to *form* a **clearer vision** of your **dreams** *within* your **mind**. And *change* your **thinking** to **grow** a **new perspective**. Because it is with **clear dreams** that you become more **confident** of what you want out of life and become **surer** of where you are **headed**.

The **object** of you *performing* these **mental exercises** will be to help you to begin **perceiving** the *world* on a more **advanced level**. So as you **perform** these **money-meditation exercises,** understand how *vitally* **important** they are to your **mental transformation**. This is vital. Why? Today we live in a **fast-paced, high-tech** world where we are constantly bombarded *day after day* with lots of **noise**. The **meditations** are *designed* to help you to begin *turning down the noise* in your **head** so that you can **increase** your *focus*. Further, they will help you to **communicate images** of your **dreams** to your **mind**. My friend, before you can **succeed,** you must see your **dreams** coming true in your **mind** first in order to begin the **process** of **making** them real! That is until you take the time-out to **define** your **dreams**. You cannot expect to go anywhere in life **fast**!

So once again, your *rise* will begin with your **dream**! So **open** your **mind** to the **money-meditation process**. It will help you to begin **flooding** your **imagination** with a **clear mental picture** of your **dream**. It is with a **clear mental picture** of your **dreams** in your **mind** that you can develop the **motivation** to go out into the world to **make your first million**! It is through this **process** of you developing your **dream** that you will get the **ball rolling**! Your **dream** will *open up* the *door* to a *new* **brighter future** where you can

rise up, shine hard, and **accumulate money** in **large amounts!** It all starts in your **mind** with your **dreams!** So **focus.** Now as you **prepare** to begin **performing** this **exercise, think** of this: First see your **dreams clearly** in your **mind** and then develop the **belief** in your **heart** that your **dream** can and will **come true.** And then go on to develop some **practical plans** to make your **dreams** real. Then everything you **dream** of can and *will* come true if you **make it happen!** Or in other words, just like a **gold medalist** on the **mission** for the **gold,** you must begin **seeing** yourself **reaching** your **million-dollar dream destination** in your *mind's eye* well before the day of its **attainment.**

Now *zoom* in and **focus!** In this chapter, you will begin developing a **vision** in your **mind** of your own **new American magazine dream.** As a **rule,** when you walk through this **process,** do not worry about going overboard. **Dream** as big and **bold** as your **heart** will allow. So do not worry about **dreaming** to **big.** Why? Because **dreaming** what may seem to be an **impossible dream** for someone else may be a very **possible dream** for you! So **think big!** And **dream** even **bigger!** And remember that in **America,** anything is **possible!** That in **America,** you can **dream** the **impossible dream!** And that in **America, impossible dreams** can become an **inevitable reality!**

Now as you *develop* your **dream** in your **mind,** it is **important** that you *remember* that **America** is the *world's* number one **land of opportunity!** Keeping this fact in **mind** will help to *open up the* door in your **mind** to begin *perceiving* all of the **opportunities** that **exist** across **America.** Through the **money-meditation process,** you will begin to *develop* in your **mind** a **money consciousness** and a **business mind.** *Developing* a **money consciousness** is where you begin to *grow* an **awareness** of all of the **money** that is **flowing around** you in your **city,** your **state,** and across **America.** *Developing* a **business mind** is where you begin to **formulate** some **specific plans** and **strategies** to *set up* **businesses** to get the **money flowing around** you. So now ask where do **dreams** come from? *Dreams* *come from and take **shape** in our **souls**. There, our **dreams** are born out of our **deepest desires, passions,** and **ambitions**. Our **desires flow** from our **souls** and move along to **flash** into our **hearts** in the form of our **passions**. Next, our **dreams** move along and **surface** in our **minds** and take **shape** as our **ambitions** and **visions** of the **future**. So the **deeper** the **desire** that **stirs** within your **soul** and the **stronger** the **passion** that your heart **receives**, then the clearer the **dream** that will **surface** in your **mind** in the form of your **ambition**.*

So to **achieve** your **million-dollar dream**, first you must stir a **desire** within yourself so **strong** that you come to **desire riches** just as strongly as you wish to **breathe**! Then you must become driven with a **deep passion** within your **heart** to **win**! And after that, you must develop a clear vision of your **dream**. So be aware that your **dream** now resides within your soul that you must awaken. And that your **imagination** is a blank canvas upon which you must paint a clear picture of this **dream**! Which brings us to the **million-dollar question**. What is your **dream**? And what will your **dream** life look like?

For the **money-meditation *Exercises*** you will need:

- ➡ A pen, pencil, or new document screen on your computer.

- ➡ A tablet of paper, or blank document screen record your thoughts.

- ➡ Then find yourself a quiet private place where you can isolate yourself from the world and think. This quiet place will become your lab where you can escape the noise, get your mind right, focus, and begin to take your dreams from the abstract to the concrete form.

- ➡ Once you are there, take the time-out to breath, relax, reflect, think, imagine, and begin the process of absorbing the thoughts of becoming a million-dollar business talent in your mind's eye.

➡ Suggestion: read this entire chapter first then go back and perform each money-meditation exercise.

➡ Note: continue performing the money-meditation exercises until you are confident that your dreams are images taking root inside of your mind. (Remember that your dream is the foundation upon which your platinum plan will be built so take your time with the process.)

Money-meditation exercise no. 1: money consciousness

Now let's begin the **process** of shaping your **magazine dreams**! First, in this **process,** you will learn to still your **mind** and focus your **thoughts** to begin the **process** of controlling your **thinking.** Follow my suggestions as completely as you can. Then **practice, practice,** and then **practice** these **money-meditation exercises** again and again. Why? Because **practice** leads to **mastery**! Lying down or sitting, close your eyes, then **focus** on relaxing and calming your breathing. Breathe deep, slow breathes in your nose and out of your mouth. With each breathe that you breathe in and out, **imagine** that the inside of your **mind** is a *giant digital clock screen* and that each time that you breathe in and out, a red number appears on the *screen* in your **mind** starting at **sixty** and counting down to **fifty-nine, fifty-eight, fifty-seven, fifty-six, fifty-five, fifty-four** until you count down to **one.** Open your **imagination**. Push all of the **thoughts** out of your **head** that distract you from this **process**. And at the point that you have counted down for a *minute or more,* your **mind** should *start* to become **still**.

At the moment that your **mind** becomes **calm,** take a few minutes to **reflect** upon your life. Rewind your *thoughts* back in time and **think** hard about the **decisions** that you have made in the past.

Imagine how your past **financial decisions** have lead you to where you are **money wise** today. **Imagine** how you would have **managed** your **finances** differently in the past and how you could possibly be in a better place today. **Think** and **Reflect**. We start here first to help you begin to **see** where you've been so you can begin the **process** of *looking* to the **future** to see *new possibilities* and **envision** how your **magazine dream** can open *new doors* of **monetary achievement** for you in the **future**.

Keep relaxing, thinking, and continue to breathe easily. And now let's go a little further to imagine your potential future following the path of entrepreneurship as your vehicle to accumulating money. Let's look ahead to the future and visualize your rise to the top! In your mind, fast forward to that future moment in your life where you become a successful, **bankable business talent**. Imagine that you followed the path of **entrepreneurship** and have become extremely successful. Think of how of how you would *feel* upon successfully **building** a **business** from the ground up where your ideas have become **income**. Imagine that your business has made you your **first million dollars**. Imagine that you have it all, you're going places, doing big things. See the vision of success clearly as you can in your mind. **Feel it, taste it, touch it, and smell it** until it becomes real in your **mind**.

Imagine that you are the **hot** new face on *television* and the *Internet*. You have thousands of **friends** and **fans** on **Facebook, Instagram,** and **Twitter**. You are in high demand. You feel beautiful and radiant. You are making **power moves** and **politicking** on your cell phone. **Imagine** yourself in the **possession** of all of the material things that your heart desires in the world. **Picture** your **dream home,** see your **dream car,** and imagine what you will **wear**, your **jewelry**, maybe a **yacht**, and a **private jet**. Whatever you can possibly **dream** of yourself having that **money** can buy, **visualize** these things *clearly* in your *mind's eye* and **believe** in your heart that you will **gain possession** of these things. **Imagine** that all your **financial** problems fade away. Visualize that your cup will runneth over **today, tomorrow,** and into **eternity**. Now once you have a *clear* **image** of your **dreams** in your **mind** of how you wish to live and how it will feel, then snap a picture of this in your **mind**. Burn this **picture** into your **imagination**.

If you have successfully completed the **money-meditation** exercises up unto this point, then it is now time for you to put a price tag on your **dream**! Placing a price tag on your **dream** is when you ask yourself what it would cost you to live the way that you have just **imagined**. And then develop a round ballpark figure of what dollar amount it would cost you to **bankroll** your **dream**. To place a price tag on your **dream**, take a moment to rewind back to bring the picture of your **dream** life back into your **mind**. Once the picture is clear mentally, begin walking through your **dream** world placing a price tag on everything that you see in your **possession**. (You can go online to do a **Google** search to get prices for all of the things that you wish for, or you can guesstimate). The **goal** is to develop a round number that will represent how much **money** you will need to **accumulate** to make your **dreams** real. **Example**: To live the lifestyle of my dreams I will need to accumulate $**10 million**. Once you have developed a round number, multiply the number by ten. This number will become your **long-term financial goal** in your **life**.

For example, if your round number is **$10 million,** then you will multiply this number by **ten**, which will equal **$100 million,** which will become your **ultimate financial goal** that you will vow to **accumulate** over the course of your lifetime. Do the math and record this dollar amount. Write your **ultimate financial goal** down now! This is how you begin to define your **dreams**. The act of recording your **dreams** in any concrete form makes your **dreams** become visible. On the occasion that your **dreams** become visible, then you can begin the process of articulating them into your **platinum plan**. Your **platinum plan** starts with the **ultimate financial goal** that you set for yourself. In the next chapter of this book, you will develop your **platinum plan** to accomplish your **magazine dream**.

But before you can create your **platinum plan,** it is imperative that you have your **ultimate financial** life **goal** in place. Why? *This process is **designed** to help you clarify your **financial intentions**. Thus beginning the process of you **transforming** your financial feelings into the **material form**.* Meaning once you have your **ultimate financial goal** in place then you are moving in the right direction to win! How? Because your **magazine dream,** once written down with a **definite** date for **achievement,** becomes an **ultimate life goal.** This **goal** further broken down into smaller baby steps will become the fabric of your **platinum plan.** Setting these **goals** and **objectives** will be your **secret weapon.** These are **vital tools** that you will need to build your **house** of **success.** (**Note:** In the beginning **stages,** keep your **dreams goals** and **plans** to yourself! Why? Because some people in your life may not **believe** in you and may even try to sabotage you).

Now at this step in the process, put the book down so that you can write down your **ultimate financial goal. Example**: Write down I (**your name**) am about to **hustle up** and stack my first $1,000,000. I will accumulate $1,000,000 by *any legit means necessary* **making money moves** *in the American* **business arena** *as a star* **entrepreneur**. *Once you have completed this step and have written down your* **ultimate financial life goal,** *then your* **goal** *is halfway reached*! How? Everything in the *form of your success will first start inside* of your **heart** and your **mind**. When you *write down your* **goals** *and* **believe** *that you can and will achieve them, then your goals become set*. The other half is when you go out and **make it happen**! So once you have a **dollar amount** written down of what you **believe,** it will cost you to **fund** your **dreams,** then now you must go further to develop a **firm** belief in your **heart** that you can and will go **achieve** your **dream**.

Having goals to accomplish your dream also makes you responsible for making them real. Your ultimate financial goals that you have articulated must be what you believe to be realistic for yourself to achieve. You must believe in your dreams and all that you set out to do before you can take the leap. The limitations that we have are usually only the ones that we place on ourselves. The key is to make your **dreams, goals,** and objectives as clear as possible. To make your ultimate financial goal more reachable, you must break your goals down into smaller, more manageable projects. Regardless of how big your **ultimate** financial goal may be, your goal here is to make your first **million.** Now you may **desire** to set your **focus** on your ultimate financial goal. Nine times out of ten, your ultimate goal is to accumulate a lot more than a million bucks.

That is quite understandable, my friend, but as I have stated in a preceding chapter, making your first million will be a **process.**

You have to learn how to crawl before you can walk. You must learn to walk before you can run. And learn to run before you can fly! Right now, your brighter future is within your reach. All you must do now to win is to keep reaching! You must follow the process. Now write down the specific date by which you desire to have your first **million** dollars in the palms of your empty hands.

DATE:

To burst forward on your road to riches, you will have to place a deadline on your dreams! So you will have to be specific about when you plan to have a million in hand.

The date that you set for your dream deadline will create a time sensitivity that will put some fire up under your behind to get up and make it happen! If you do not set a deadline, there is a strong chance that you may never get the nerve up to get started. By attaching a deadline to each, and every one of your long-term as well as short-term **goals,** you help ensure that you will eventually take the actions that will lead you to reach each and every one of your goals in real time. With **prior** proper **planning** and setting goals, you can gradually progress. The process of accumulating money is the process that you must harness to climb the ladder of success. The process of accumulating money is the day-to-day goals that you set where you generate money day after day until you achieve your million-dollar dream. As you write down your goals and deadlines of your dream, pay close attention to how you feel inside. You may have some fear, anxiety, and doubt at first.

If you feel any of these **feelings,** know that these feelings are quite natural. You are entering a new place mentally, and we tend to fear the unknown. If you follow the steps in this book, I will show you how you can begin to look inside yourself and locate all that you will need to be strong to pursue your dreams with conflunce. In time, all your fears and **doubts** will begin to melt away. It is the **faith** and **belief** in your **heart** that your **dreams** will someday come true that will drive you to overcome your **fears.** You must overcome your fears because it is our fears that will ultimately stand in the way of you making your dreams a reality in the **future.** Through overcoming your **fears,** you will be able to face the world with faith and confidence. You cannot win with a timid heart.

You must **trust** and believe that you will touch a **million** dollars in your lifetime.

Push all feelings of fear and doubt out of yourself now! Know that you will have what you strive for in this life! Believe that you will gain a **million** dollars if you strive for a **million!** Be confident knowing that your financial **condition** will change in life when you yourself change your **condition** by following your dreams! Allow this **thinking** to serve as the foundation of your drive and determination to win in the game! This mode of **thinking** will help you tap in to unlock your inner potential to use the power of your mind to do great things! This process is equal to when a sperm drop reaches a fertile egg in the womb setting the process of childbirth in motion. Only you are impregnating your mind with essential thoughts to set the process of your rise to the top in motion. Just as an egg that has been fertilized gradually develops and grows within the womb until one day it is born. By following these mental instructions herein, the same thing will happen with these dreams of riches that you are planting in your **mind.**

These ideas will begin to grow inside of your mind until they spill over and give birth to your platinum plans and strategies that will take your dreams from the abstract to the concrete. This is your money consciousness taking form. The first money-consciousness exercise was designed to help you begin to burn a visual image of you achieving *riches into your mind*. The object is to accelerate the process of you developing a clear picture of your dreams in your **mind**. As with any **form** of exercise if performed properly, you will begin to get stronger over time. Your mind muscles shall begin to grow until you become mentally stronger. So every day from this point forward, I would suggest that you set aside some time to practice this **money-**meditation exercise until your magazine dream is all that you see! Let's keep it moving along!

Money meditation exercise **no. 2: business** mind

Now let's begin the process of developing your business **mind!** This is the process of you turning your vision to begin **thinking** like a **boss!** To begin **thinking** like a **boss,** let's imagine that you have a million cash in your bank account at this moment.

Imagine what you would do with a million dollars in cash today. How would you spend your newfound riches? **Think.** This is a financial issue that you will have to address as a boss. As a **boss,** you will have to deal with how you will allocate **funds** continuously such as how you would save some of the money. Would you invest a portion of the money to make it grow? If so, how would you invest the money? Would you go on a shopping spree to buy out the mall, purchase a new car, and buy all that your heart desires?

Learning the power of a **dollar** is where you begin to be aware of the many different ways that you can invest your **money** to make it **grow.** Your business **mind** should always look for new opportunities to expand and grow your money and assets! This is your business **mind** taking shape. Now imagine yourself running a million-dollar operation that is generating money in large amounts! Cast any fears aside that may surface in your mind. Remember that this is only a mental exercise. If you can't see yourself running a million-dollar operation, then how can you expect others to see it as well? Believe in yourself! Look inside yourself and be strong! There is a millionaire inside of you waiting to be born! See yourself getting paid big money! (If you have made it this far in the process, then you shall have already developed some basic key information that will serve as the foundation of your platinum plan). Congratulations!

ISHMAIL HAMED

The New American Dream Job!

In recent news! It seems that we have entered a new **age** in **American** history where a new **American dream** is being **ushered** in. The buzz about the **new American *magazine dream*** has people across America positively euphoric! The **new American *magazine* dream** is the dream of **rising up, shining hard,** and accumulating **money** in large amounts in ways not seen in yesteryears!

After a spell of widespread economic ills due to the recession, many **Americans** have discovered a new **American dream** job through the process of creating **businesses** that they own and control. This is the new popular investment vehicle people are using to make their **magazine** dreams come true! With this method, **Americans** are **re-restructuring** their investments, breathing new life into their finances, and resetting their **incomes.** This group of **Americans** are becoming **millionaires** in record time! It seems people are regaining **financially** what in recent years they had lost.

Due to this new development among the **entrepreneurial** class, the annual growth rate of our economy has risen nearly 1/3 percent in the last year. The Dow **Jones Industrial** Average is soaring due to new consumer confidence! Further, through this widespread embracement of the **entrepreneurial spirit, a** new record number of jobs are being created in the **private** sector!

And it seems, at last, the hunger of the **American** Consumer has been aroused once again, and in effect, opening up the floodgates to record-breaking consumer spending in the retail sector not witnessed in years!

And now the Fed has forecasted that our **American** economy is positioned to grow at a steady rate of 5–10 percent or more annually over the span of the next ten to twenty years! At this rate, our economy can possibly double, if not triple, in size by the year **2035!**

(This news column is a work of fiction designed to stimulate thought). Imagine that! Let's go!

Chapter 3

Platinum Plans!

The world is yours and everything in it! At this point, you shall have reached a turning point in your life where the brighter future of your dreams is mentally within your reach and has begun to take shape! Through following the money-meditation process, you should now have a clearer vision of your magazine dreams in your mind! Developing your magazine dream was the first lap on your money-motivated mission. To begin the next lap in taking your dreams from the abstract to the concrete form, you must formulate a precise set of practical plans for making your magazine dreams real! I call this process platinum planning. In this chapter, you will begin sketching and building your **platinum** plans for making your first million!

You must know that there are a multitude of people across the world that desire to live a life of fame and riches. But what generally separates the haves from the have nots is the specific plans for accumulating wealth that each adopts in their life. There is a saying that goes "Most people **do not plan to** fail in life; rather, they just fail to plan." The same goes for you! Recognize that no matter how smart or intelligent that you imagine yourself to be, you will not advance very far on the road to riches without a definite set of practical plans. So if you truly desire to succeed in the money game, you must first develop a master plan to win! Your platinum plan is your master plan that will open the door for you to begin transforming your life from rags to riches!

Taking the time-out to create a set of clear-cut, practical plans for achieving your dreams is possibly one of the most important things that you will ever do in life. This is a turning point where your life can begin to change for the better. But before you can begin creating your **platinum** plan there are some things about the process that you must learn. On one hand, **creating** your platinum plan will help increase your chances of **success!** While on the flip side, if you do not take the time-out to create your plan before embarking on your million-dollar **mission,** you will almost be guaranteeing that you will fail. Now as you know, you can possibly accumulate your first million dollars without putting a plan in place. But why try such a thing, huh? Give me one good reason why you would attempt to do something like that. Let's get your platinum **plan** together. Whenever you take a journey of any sort, before moving along your way, it is a prudent choice to acquire a road map that will help illuminate your path ahead.

Obtaining your own road map to guide you toward your million-dollar destination is a fundamental step you must take before embarking upon your journey! Your platinum **plan** is your very own road map to success that is tailor-made to your life! Your **map** will be your guide to point you in the right direction. At any given moment along the way, your map will be able to gauge your progress and show you if you are headed the right way or not. This map will **guide** you from point **A to point money!** When **planning,** remember that the **focus** of the platinum **planning** process is for you to create flexible plans that will work for you! So create your plans with an open mind, which will allow you space to create intelligent, flexible plans. Intelligent, **flexible** plans take into consideration that nothing in this life is ever set in stone, and to the future, we are blind.

Intelligent, flexible plans are always new, fresh, green, ever-changing, and in tune with the *current* times. With intelligent, flexible plans in place on the road ahead, you will provide yourself ample room to adapt and change in the face of anything that life may throw your way. Creating intelligent plans will help you to avoid your plans being set back, avoid a great deal of unforeseen problems, and make your every move a calculated step. When you get into the habit of thinking forward and planning ahead, you gain a new degree of power and control over your destiny and your life. This is the structure of a solid platinum plan. Your platinum plan is your career plan that will govern your business life. Creating your platinum plan will start the process of you thinking things through and writing out your life's mission statement. Your life's mission statement or your vision of success describes all of your financial goals and objectives that you wish to reach in life.

Making your first million is the **focus** of your platinum plan and your immediate financial goal. Within the structure of your platinum plan will be a series of smaller plans and goals in the form of business ventures that will help you move closer to your million-dollar goal step by step. You will have to start **looking** into the world to locate business opportunities with your new money consciousness and business **mind.** You must find businesses that you can invest in that have the potential to make you rich. Each business venture that you invest in will be a vehicle that you shall use to achieve millionaire status! As I stated before with all of the financial ills of our day, you can possibly get rich building businesses around the demand that this new market creates! (You must accumulate **money by** any **legit** means necessary to rise)!

I call this your **platinum** plan because in the **music** business, when you sell a million records, you go platinum. So I say in the business arena as a star entrepreneur, when you make a million bucks, your **plans** go platinum! Your platinum **plan** is your master plan for taking over and making your first million! It is your plan to blow up and break out on the scene to rise to become a bankable star entrepreneurial talent!

Your **platinum** plan will help you when you need to make **big** decisions and power moves! Your plan will illustrate to you when and how you should reorganize your strategies. Your plan will also help **guide** and direct you on what necessary course of action that you will need to take when you begin to expand and grow in the future. But never forget that no matter how big you may possibly get, without a plan in place on the road ahead, you run the serious risk of crashing and going down big like the *Titanic*.

Your platinum **plan** is the starting point in your rise to the top!

The planning process is a process of trial and error. Have patience. It is a tedious process, but you must not be discouraged. Follow the **process** through to the end. It is a possibility that you may have to change your plans in the future. Sometimes you may even need to go so far as completely scrapping your first plan and start the process of creating a new plan. So now the time has come. It is time for you to draw out the first copy of your **platinum** plan. From this moment forward, you must dedicate yourself to the planning process and be willing to do whatever it takes to win! Do not worry about doing it wrong. Just do it! I will show you how. Take your time. This will be worth every minute of your time if your plan helps you become a millionaire! Remember that the goal for you is to create an intelligent, flexible **plan** that works! Read on!

Welcome to the millionaires mind technology software process! To be logical, **realistic,** and practical through the process of creating your platinum plan, I want to introduce you to the process in a *manner that helps you reduce* your planning risk and help to increase your **likelihood** of success! Even though there are no hard rules for rising to fortune and fame in the world. The rules that I am herein setting forth are worth serious consideration. The **guiding** rules to construct your **platinum** plan:

1. Think forward. And then write out your vision of success.

2. Do your research, gather the *necessary* facts, and consider your options.

3. Decide which business you will invest in to start building your profit portfolio.

THE ART OF MAKING MONEY

4. Set your goals. And clarify your objective strategies!

5. Execute your **platinum** plan. Monitor your progress! Then adjust.

➡ Get hold of something to record your **platinum** plan with such as a pen and paper, or a new document screen on your computer.

➡ Revisit your quiet place where you can think, connect, and construct your platinum plan.

➡ Record your ultimate financial goal here: $_____

The first step in the platinum-**planning** process is you thinking ahead. Once you begin thinking ahead, you will then write out and state a clear vision of what level of success that you hope to achieve in the long term over the course of your life here on earth. It is important to have a clear vision of your magazine dreams in your mind when creating your platinum plan. You should have a clear vision of your **magazine** dreams in your mind at this time. Know that your dreams are no more than mere imaginings without some solid plan and strategies to make them happen. Your vision of success is how you plan to achieve your magazine dream step-by-step. Your vision of success is what I call your life's **mission** statement. Your life's **mission** statement is generally what you believe to be your purpose here on earth. It is a detailed description of how you plan to enter the money game, take control, corner, and dominate your chosen markets.

Your vision of success will help guide you as you research and examine each of the many possible avenues that you may take that will serve as the ways and means that are appropriate for accomplishing your goals and objectives. So now to begin the process of giving shape to your **vision of** success, you must answer a few questions such as what is it that you dream of becoming? What is your ultimate vision of success? Where do you see yourself ten to twenty years in the future financially? How will you get there? What is it that you believe to be your calling in life? How do you imagine that you can begin from where you are in life to begin transforming your life from rags to riches? (Understand that no matter what your actual dream may be, as an entrepreneur you can accumulate enough **money** to spend on making any of your dreams come true!)

Take the time-out now to **think** about your future. See yourself rising to **success! Think** forward to develop a clear vision of where you are headed. Be confident in yourself, in your abilities, and **confident** in who you are and where you are headed in life. Your vision of success will aid you in gaining the confidence that you need. When you step into the shadow of the American entrepreneur, you open the door in your life to start financially prospering and **growing** in ways that you may have recently thought **impossible.** To begin the process, you must develop a vision of the financial world where you fully grasp economic issues of the world big and small. The aim is for you to develop a money consciousness and **a business mind** that you will use to determine where the big *money* is flowing, then create businesses to compete for these dollars that exist in the markets of your focus. You must zoom your mind's lens out to observe the big picture of America and the world as a whole. Then you must *zoom* back in to look at the details of the local markets in your state, your region, and your city to find cash **sources** that you can **build businesses** around.

America offers everyone who lives within her borders almost **limitless** opportunities to rise as high as our *talents* and *intelligence* will allow us to go competing in the free market **business** arena. Right now, you have everything laid out in front of you in the American free market system that you need to get rich! In every city across America from the East Coast to the West Coast, there is money and opportunity always ready and waiting to respond to the demands of a hustling go-getter with **big** dreams and a plan! When you appear on the scene, there will already be players in the game winning. What will set you apart from everyone in the game is your **vision of** success and your **plan.**

To set in motion your campaign of dominating the business arena, you have to start **thinking** real **big**, dreaming big, and planning even bigger! Try this: Imagine now a vision of your city. Do not see your city through the eyes of a consumer or a working citizen but see your city through the eyes of a conqueror and as a star entrepreneur. You must enter the business arena with the attitude of Alexander the Great! Only your dream is to become a great entrepreneur. As an entrepreneur, you will connect with your local community by setting up businesses in your city to attract the local dollars that are flowing from your city's *business financial centers* to your bank accounts. You must find something hot to offer a group of people for sell and develop plans around these to get the money! As **a money-conscious, business-**minded entrepreneur, you can stay on the alert to recognize open or hidden voids that you can fill to satisfy one of the many hungers of the American consumer market.

These are what you will develop your platinum plan around. You must look into the world to locate lucrative business opportunities that you can exploit. Getting in on the business end of rising markets is how you will make **money.** I suggest that you create your plan around new rising markets. The secret to your success lies in how well you can uncover new rising markets that you can set up businesses around. When looking for new rising markets, be open-minded, flexible, and willing to adapt, which will allow you to exploit any of the opportunities that you may discover. You can exploit these new rising markets by introducing merchandise with a strong demand that consumers can devour. The formula to win: when business booms, you must hustle, stack, and save the money, then reinvest in additional business ventures to continue to grow.

Now put pen to the paper to record your vision of success, or create a new computer file labeled my vision of success. (Write out and describe your vision of success in as few words as possible.)

There are no **hard rules** when **looking into** potential businesses that you may possibly invest in. But there are some valuable resources that you can employ when seeking valuable information. In today's world, we live in what is called the Information Age. It is called the Information Age due to the vast amount of information that is available to us today through mass mediums such as the Internet. The Internet places the world at our fingertips. Whatever information that we can possibly conceive of can be obtained through a Google search, a Microsoft's Bing search, or maybe even a Yahoo! search.

But when searching for precise business knowledge to investigate any business that you may be interested in investing in, there are some key places that you can get good information.

Universities and colleges have individuals on their staff who can give you assistance concerning new business start-ups. The chamber **of *commerce*** may help you with specific business issues. Another place to gather valuable information is the small business administration. It is an agency that our government has set up to help entrepreneurs. This organization is ideal for providing you with information that can help you to perform your investigation on any business you may want to invest in. (I suggest that you go online and Google the small business administration. Take a look at their SCORE office.) Decide which business ventures to invest in:

---

1. Do your homework.

2. Gather facts.

3. Consider your options.

Here, I have selected twenty business fields for you to study. Study these to gather some facts. Then consider your options. You may find other business fields outside of these options during your investigation. These are just a starting point:

1. Arts and crafts

2. Audio and visual production

3. Automotive repair services

4. Beauty salons/barbershops

5. Business consultants

6. Cleaning services (commercial, industrial, and residential)

7. Clothing design

8. Communications consultants

9. Computer services/repair

10. Construction

11. Entertainment professionals

12. Financial consultants

13. General contractors

14. Internet businesses owners

15. Investment brokers

16. Landscaping contractors

17. Life coach experts

18. New Age marketing firms

19. Promotions companies

20. Real estate investors

Once you have done your homework, gathered your facts, and considered your options, you must decide which **business** ventures you will invest in to kick off what I have labeled your profit **portfolio!** You will start from the bottom and hustle your way to the top! So from this point forward, if you are going to rise to riches, you are going have to get into the game and hustle, hustle, then hustle harder! You will have to zone in and decide which businesses you will invest in to generate some income! Each **business** venture that you invest in will be a potential stream or streams of income that will grow into your profit portfolio! You will invest in any of the numerous legitimate business ventures that entrepreneurs across America and the world invest in to make some dough. Your profit **portfolio** will be an assortment of the business ventures that you choose. This will be your specific ways and means for generating yourself some streams of income to make your first million!

Acquiring business that you own and control whether it is a new business start-up, or you buy an existing business that is already generating positive cash flow, or maybe you buy into a lucrative franchise opportunity, or develop a strategic partnership with a business ally that you align yourself with to prosper! It does not really matter which field of business that you pursue as long as you can establish a solid stream of income, make some profits, and begin to save some money. On the whole, the objective of your platinum plan is to discover ways to invest your money to build yourself a business empire that over time will generate you a **million** bucks. As a creative thinker, you must uncover new markets that you can conquer and take over. Then create platinum plans to claim your newly discovered business territory!

To begin formulating your campaign strategy to take over, start by taking a mental look at your city as a whole. Ask yourself where the money is flowing in large **amounts** through your city. Now turn your attention to look to the downtown area. **Downtown** is usually the financial center of a **city.** The downtown area in a city is usually where you will find all of the things of importance that you may need to purchase. This is why entrepreneurs set up businesses downtown to attract the local dollars from the local community's purses and wallets. But every city is unique, so downtown may not always necessarily be the financial center of a **city.** It is your job to find out where the **money** is flowing. Then there are the rare occasions when you may live in a **city** where there is a serious lack of money flowing. There is a simple solution to solve this problem. Move! To win, you must be willing to sacrifice and go to where the money is at! If you find that there is no **money** flowing in your city, keep this in mind.

The more time you spend in a **broken** town, the longer you will be **broke!** If this is your case, then take a lesson from the people of the gold rush days who migrated to the West to pursue their dreams of riches! You must find out where the money is at and get after it with **NASCAR** speeds! Another idea is that you can stay put and hustle on the Internet. For the computer savvy, there is a **flood** of ways to accumulate money online. Websites such as Amazon offer a forum which allows you to do business on their website. This may be the perfect method for you to get into the game and make some real **dough** in real time! There are many forms of financial opportunity online. If you have a mind for business, the opportunities online are limitless! You must investigate all of your **options** to locate what will work for you! Let's keep it moving!

Setting your platinum plans goals. Now once you have done your homework, have gathered your facts, considered your options, and have decided which business opportunity you will invest in, it will be time for you to *zoom* in to form and set the goals in your platinum plan. To fashion a *winning* platinum plan for yourself, you will need to learn the art of setting and reaching financial goals in your life. Why? The goals that you set here will give your life direction. Each goal that you *develop* will be a specific step that you will need to take along the road ahead to make your **magazine** dreams a reality. Setting the goals in your platinum plan will give your dreams shape! So make each of the goals that you set as clear as possible! Why? The clearer the goals that you set, the easier that each goal can be used as a light and a guide to illuminate the road ahead on your **money-motivated mission!** Clear **goals** allow you to make cool, calculated power money moves with a clear focus behind them!

Now you will begin the process of *writing* your goals down. Here, you must *write* down your short-term as well as your long-term goals that you *hope* to achieve in your life.

Each goal should be a specific step that you will need to take in your life now and into the future financially **step by** step to achieve your dream goal. Example goals: *Your* **goal** *in life today is to* **make** *your* **first million***! Once I get rich, one of my* **goals** *is to buy a huge luxury home filled with furniture imported from Paris. The whole house will be laced with white Italian carpet throughout. My home will also have an* **Olympic-sized swimming pool** *in the backyard as well as a fleet of the finest luxury cars my garage. Another of my* **goals** *once I get rich is* **to travel the world** *and the* **seven seas!**

Whatever your magazine dreams are made of, you must write them down now. When writing down your **goals,** I suggest that you develop each of your **goals** for the **long-term** as well as your short-term goals in three dimensions. The three-dimensional goal-setting process is that when you set a goal, (1) you set an optimistic component to your goal, (2) you set a pessimistic component to your goal, and (3) finally, you set a realistic component of that same goal. The process of creating three-dimensional goals opens the door for you to have a more efficient method for gauging your progress and measuring each level of success that you attain. This process will be a vital tool that you can use for making better **decisions** and creating more practical plans in the future.

- When setting a goal, the best-case scenario that you envision where you reach the highest level of success and progress that is potentially available to you within each particular situation is called the optimistic component.

- When setting a goal, the worst-case scenario that you envision where you reach the lowest level of success and progress that is potentially available to you within each particular situation is called the pessimistic component.

- When setting a goal, the real case scenario where you arrive at the actual level of success and progress that was potentially available to you within that particular situation is called the realistic component.

Now write down your goals! (Remember, your goals are general statements of how you will achieve your magazines dreams step-by-step! Make your goals as clear as possible to help guide you.)

1. My goal is to hustle up and make my first million by any legit means necessary!

2. _____

3. _____

4. _____

THE ART OF MAKING MONEY

5. _____
   _____

6. _____
   _____

7. _____
   _____

8. _____
   _____

9. _____
   _____

10. _____
    _____

Clarify your objective strategies. Now you will spell out your objective strategies, describing the specific actions that you plan to take to reach each goal that you have set in your platinum plan. Your objective strategies should match up exactly and carry each goal that you plan to achieve. These objective strategies must be precise, measurable statements of the specifics of each of your goals. Keep in mind that every strategy you select will be unique. As with your **goals** you set, the aim with your strategies is to make them as clear as possible to help guide you. Your goals and strategies are the links in the chain within the structure of your platinum plan, which will move you closer to your million-dollar goal little by little. When formulating your strategies, the more **options** you have available to you, the better. Through the process, you must consider all of your potential **options** before formulating your strategies. But regardless of your financial situation, you must learn to utilize what you have got!

The strategies you create are vital to your success, so be smart! Your aim is to develop **strategies** that work! When moving forward, your objective strategies will serve as a tool to measure your success and progress within each given situation. The strategies that you develop are a tool that helps you to focus your three most important resources, which are your **time, energy**, and **money.** By **focusing** your three most important resources, you can gain maximum results from your efforts in the least amount of time. This can help you avoid losing your resources on a **trial-**and-error basis. Thus, reducing the amount of resources that you waste can lead to **increased** profits, which can lead to you making a million dollars faster! Also, developing solid strategies to achieve your goals can raise the number of wins that you put under your belt off the top! Let's go!

THE ART OF MAKING MONEY

Now clarify an objective strategy to match each goal you have set in your platinum plan! (Remember to make your objective strategies as clear as possible. Take all of the time that you need to complete this step in the process.)

1. I will invest in such and such business venture to begin the process of achieving my goal of making my first million.

2. _____

3. _____

4. _____

5. _____

6. _____

7. _____

8. _____

9. _____

10. _____

Upon successfully **defining** your goals and clarifying your objective strategies in your **platinum** plan, you must execute your plan without delay! My friend, listen closely. Once your goals and **objective** strategies have been developed, set your platinum plan in motion immediately! Start doing everything within your power to begin making things happen today. Never wait for tomorrow or the right time to get started executing your **plans.** Why? Because if you wait and drag your feet, you will run the risk of never getting started on making your platinum plans a reality at all! This is the truth. The idea is to set your plans in motion today and then keep them in motion until you make a million dollars! Once things get moving along, you must implement a system that will help you to monitor your progress. Monitoring your plan periodically can help you adjust your plans and strategies as new more practical information becomes available to you. This is the **process** so **focus.**

Remember that in a previous chapter, you set a target date for when you see yourself achieving your goal of accumulating your first million dollars. Here, you will write that target date down again to embed this date within the fabric of your platinum plan.

Write down the target date for **accumulating** your first **million** dollars now!

Example: I plan to have a **million** dollars in my bank account that I have generated from my **business** activities by January 1, 2030.

➡ Date: _____

Three chief reasons describing why you must set your target date:

1.	Measure and track the progress that you make along the way toward achieving your platinum plan!
2.	To supply you with the day-to-day **motivation** that you will need to continue pushing forward through the ups and downs on the road ahead.
3.	To help you to keep your eyes on your million-dollar prize until victory is won!

Next in the process. After you have set your target date for accumulating your first million dollars, you must then set a midway date to begin implementing the system of **monitoring** your progress. This midway date should be projected six months into the future from the actual date that your platinum plan is complete. This monitoring system will be a tool for checking the status of your plan. By checking the status of your plan midway after its implementation and every six months thereafter, you can assure that your plans stay on track. This system will help you make sure that your plans are on schedule and moving in the right direction. Also, this system will help you regularly step back to evaluate your plans and adjust them accordingly. Write your midway date for monitoring the progress of your platinum plan down ASAP!

➡ Midway Date: _____

From this point forward, you have got to get into a habit of **studying** your platinum plan daily. You must continuously **study** your platinum plan until you commit your plan to memory. **Uploading** your platinum plan into your memory will equip you with the mind technology needed to assist you in seeing the world through the eyes of a money-conscious, businesses-minded individual. You will need this mind-set on the road ahead to advance. So when traveling into the world daily, you must carry visions of your dreams and plans in your mind to help you to start moving closer to achieving your aspirations! Further, you have to adopt the habit of consulting your platinum plan prior to making financial decisions big and small. Your platinum plan is your blueprint for success so use it! Remember that you did not create your platinum plan to have it sitting around and collecting dust. It is the road map that will illuminate the way on your chosen path. Carrying your platinum plan in your mind daily will also help you to begin to take advantage of the opportunities that will open up to you!

As I have stated, you must set your **plan** in motion and keep it in motion until it gains the necessary momentum that you will need to generate the stream or streams of income that will grow to become your **profit** portfolio! This is your platinum plan taking form. If you have made it this far through the process, you have now reached a milestone in the millionaires **mind** technology process! Well done! Soon I will introduce you to more technical business knowledge that you will need to get into the game. Remember, all forms of success take form on the inside of your mind first before they can manifest in the material form. Now to fully complete the psychological transformation process, you must get your **mind right!** Let's go!

Looking Forward

There are *numerous reasons* for being apprehensive in today's economy when contemplating whether to invest in a new business or not. But you must always remember that America still remains the *world's* number one *undisputed* land of **opportunity! Trust** and believe that over the long-term the *potential* to *prosper* **competing** in the American business arena will be very much intact. Today with a skilled eye, you can look and see that the *weakness* in today's *national marketplace characterizes* a great sea of business **opportunity** for any patient, **shrewd, money-**conscious, business-**minded** entrepreneurial persons. When looking forward, I believe that one day, we will look back and see that any economic *decline* of today was a *necessary* **bust** cycle that was *needed* to *refresh* the American market economy so that it can continues its run! **Looking forward,** you will also see that beyond the historical potential in the U.S. economy, there are *clear reason* to be *optimistic!* Why? With the birth of a *new wave* of business starups across America, there will be *increased financial activity,* which leads to more jobs! Which will fuel new demand for new products and services to **satisfy** the **appetites** of the American consumer, which will lead to more consumer spending. Which in turn will translate into a more robust, **thriving** economy! Let's go!

Chapter 4
Get Your Mind Right!

Take a minute out of your time now to picture this. Imagine that you are standing before the doorway of your dreams! Imagine that if you open up this door, money in the amounts that you wish for will begin flowing into your life! Now envision that the doorway of your dreams is a **door** that exist somewhere in your **mind.** Now try closing your eyes to imagine this **door.** See it, touch it, and feel it. Now once the door becomes a *clear* picture in your mind, then open the door. Look through the door. Then step inside. Take a look around. What would you find? Now if you were able to walk into the future of your dreams right now today, what would your life look like? What do you see? What would you eat? How would you dress? How would you feel? How would you live? And what steps are you taking today to make your dreams a **reality?**

Think at the *moment* in your life that you make a *conscious* decision to begin striving to make your dreams a reality, then at that *time,* you will be separating yourself from the crowd. And it is at this spot in your life you will become one of the chosen few! How? In the money game, the chosen ones choose themselves! The winners in the game make a conscious decision to get into the game and **win!** So now to begin moving **forward** at an *accelerated pace* on the **road** to riches, you must prepare your mind to begin **thinking** in new ways that you may never have in the past! So let's get your mind right so that you can begin to *rise, shine,* and *accumulate money* in *large* amounts!

Now let's get your brain in the game! FOCUS. Through the creation of your platinum plan you now have a blueprint you can use as a guide to build your dreams. So each day forward to get your wheels rolling, make it a part of your everyday routine to take some time-out to study your plan! And as you study your platinum plan, never *view* it as an inert, lifeless collection of words. Rather, view it as a tool that can help breathe *new* life into your **finances.** Specifically *view* your platinum plan as a blueprint for **building** your house of success from the ground up! Now *zoom* in to consider this. Every building in this *world* that has been **built** to last was first **built** upon a strong foundation. So as with every **building,** your house of success must be **built** upon a strong foundation. The **foundation** that your **house** of success will be **built** upon is your thinking. *Through* the *pages* of this *book*, your **thinking** should have begun to **shift** in a new direction. Your **mind** should now be *pregnant* with *new* **optimism,** confidence, and faith of a new brighter future that your platinum plan has now *opened up to* you!

In this chapter, you will be **introduced** to a psychological process to develop a new perspective in your mind that can *perhaps translate* into more success coming into your life. To start this process, I will instruct you to first go take a good look in the mirror.

Why? Before you can win in the money game, you first must come to know thyself. How can knowing yourself aid you in accumulating money in large amounts you may ask? **Think.** On the road ahead, many *obstacles* will possibly stand in the way of your progress. These *obstacles* will *take shape* in the *form* of any negative people, situations, or circumstances that will *show up in your life*. But the **biggest** obstacle that will *possibly* stand in the way of your success is you! This is *unadulterated* **truth.**

Now never be so naive as to believe that just because you have created a **platinum** plan to win that all your life's financial problems will *magically* fade away. No, not at all. Why? All of the days of your life leading up to this *present* moment, you have been adopting copious amounts of **thoughts** from your **family, friends, influential** people, and your life's environments, which have shaped your perceptions of things financial. These are the thoughts that now serve as the foundation of your thinking when it comes to money. These **thoughts** that you have adopted along the way have developed into your money habits. Now some of the thought processes that you have picked up may be good and can help you to progress and rise. While at the same some, other negative ways of **thinking** that you have adopted over the years may be destructive and can lead you to financial ruin. So in this chapter, to prepare you for your money-motivated mission, you will need to get **your mind right!** The process of getting your mind right is the practice of taking some time-out in your life to do some *soul*-searching, deep **thinking,** and reflecting to study yourself and **upgrade** your **thinking.**

To make your first million you must train yourself to discipline your thinking and to discipline your actions! Why? Self-discipline is the foundation of a strong hustle, which will lead to money accumulation while having a lack of self-discipline will manifest itself in the form of reckless spending and other destructive behaviors. So if you can't develop enough self-discipline to manage your money and control your spending habits, then you are *doomed* from the get-go! Thus, to begin the *process* of upgrading your thinking, you must start examining your financial behaviors to uncover any positive habits that you have and to weed out any negative habits that you have.

This is a key fact. Why? Because at the *root* of most of the destructive financial habits you may have adopted through your life is a lack of **self-discipline.** Beyond the **negative** effects on your finances that the habits you adopt in life will have further in business having a lack of self-discipline can either *inspire* respect or disgust in people. Inspiring respect in people that you conduct business with will be a key ingredient to your success. **Think.** The first impression that you make upon potential customers and employees will have a direct effect on your company's bottom line. So it should be clear to see that there are various reasons to get your mind right before you invest any of your time, energy, or money in bringing your platinum plan to life. It is my **contention** that you have to be **psychologically** prepared to receive **large amounts** of money in your life. Why? Large amounts of money, if placed in the wrong hands of a person riddled with destructive habits, can get very messy really quickly. How many times has someone you know personally received a large lump sum of money only to blow it all because their mind wasn't in the right place? Don't let this happen to you!

The tendency a majority of people have is to jump into the money game headfirst without **thinking** ahead because they are eager to get started on **making** some money. The problem is that these types never actually take the time-out to step back and take a *real good look* at themselves before **jumping** into the game. This is a *crucial mistake* you must avoid. For further proof of this fact, ask yourself this question. How many rich and famous stars have you witnessed *fall from grace* due to their destructive habits? Most of these stars *fall from grace* because they never took the time-out to get **their mind right** and work through their contradictions before their rise to fortune and fame.

So know this. If you lack self-discipline in the money game, then you will lose more *times* than you win. That is until you get your **mind right!** So get **your mind right** today or pay the price later! Now as I have previously stated to begin this process, you must first get to know yourself. Through my research, I have found that there are two ways that are most effective through which we *learn* about our *inner selves*. **Number** one: we learn ourselves through our *experiences*. And number *two:* we *learn* about our *inner selves* through **study.** Here, we will focus on *learning* through the **study** of **books.** So which book should you read first? You may ask. Envision that there is a book of your life that now exists that is all about you. And in this book, you can study all of the people, places, and things that have shaped and influenced the way that you **think** today. Now imagine that every page of the **book** of your life now exists within your **mind,** in your memory, and within your imagination. At this moment, go find a place where you can do some soul-searching, deep **thinking,** and reflecting to **study** yourself.

While performing this mental exercise, try picturing in your mind that the book of your life is a book of mirrors. Visualize that every page in this book is a different mirror reflecting back at you a different angle and aspect of your character. The goal here is for to begin **pinpointing** the root causes of any destructive habits that you have formed and to begin to ridding yourself of these. This psychological exercise will allow you to **mentally** step outside of yourself to begin seeing yourself as other people in the world perceive you. **Think.** It is a rare and unique individual whom can *step outside* of themselves and see themselves as others do. This process will help you to begin mastering yourself and molding yourself into the ultimate you that you can possibly be!

It's all set in motion when you turn around to look inside of yourself. Then you take a **long, hard look** in the mirror and reflect upon what you see. Imagine this. On the road ahead, for you to elevate your game and play at the highest levels, it is very important for you to perfect this process of taking a step back to look at yourself and attempt to see yourself as other do. Taking an honest look at your self is essential to making yourself a success! A person who is capable of this level of sincere self-reflection is destined to excel! So when you do, take a look at yourself. If when you are looking at yourself you actually like what you see, and you truly believe that your mind is in the **right** place, then don't change. But on the flip side, if when you take a look at yourself and this time you actually do not like what you see, and the person that you are does not look like what you imagine yourself to look like when your shine is turned all the way up, then it is time for you to punch the clock because you have some serious work to do!

Here, I have developed a set of questions that will help you to begin opening your **mind.** I suggest that you ponder and reflect upon each question. These questions are designed to help you begin to illuminate your mind and set in motion the process of you reading yourself. Be honest with yourself when answering these questions so that you can become psychologically whole. This process will help you to take an honest look at the **troubled areas** of your **character** that you will need to **work** on to begin transforming yourself into becoming the star entrepreneurial talent that you need to become to make it! Once you have completed this chapter of the **psychological** transformation *process,* then you will be ready to put the key in the ignition and take **flight!** So now let's get your mind right so that you can get your shine right!

THE ART OF MAKING MONEY

Now I will present you with some mind technology questions designed to help you begin the self-reflection process. The sole aim for you to answer these questions is for you to gain knowledge of self. Specifically you have to look for any flaws in your character that may exist. Then you must uproot any flaws that that may exist in your character. You have to eliminate these flaws before they can affect your success. Think, ponder, and reflect upon each of these questions now:

1. Do you generally have a positive or negative outlook on life?

2. Are you normally optimistic or pessimistic when it comes to your money and finances?

3. What positive habits do you possess that can help you make money?

4. What destructive habits do you possess that perhaps can bring you down?

5. Do you have a mind for business?

6. Are you smart with money?

7. Do you spend money irresponsibly?

8. Are you goal-orientated?

9. Do you let fear and doubt govern your thinking?

10. Are you capable of taking the necessary actions that you need to take in order to build your success?

11. Do you take careful calculated risks?

12. Or are you the impulsive type that takes a lot of unnecessary risks?

13. Do you surround yourself with trustworthy, dependable, loyal people?

14. Or do you surround yourself with sharks and cutthroats?

15. Do you think that people in the public would rather do business with a solid person full of charter?

16. Or do you imagine that people would rather do business with a person lacking in character and integrity?

17. Are you a leader?

18. Or are you a follower?

19. Are you a person who drags their feet and puts things off?

20. Or are you a self-starter who gets the job done?

21. Do you follow projects through that you have started to completion?

22. Or have you left a trail of many unfinished projects in your past?

23. When conducting business, do you give people their money's worth?

24. Or do you seek to shortchange people and get over?

25. Do you have in approachable personality that is favorable to attracting business, or are you shut off? How will this influence your business dealings?

26. Are you open-minded, flexible, **and** willing **to change** when it comes to embracing new concepts, new ideas, and

doing things in a new or different way than you are accustomed to?

27. Do you take action without obtaining solid information and facts to support your decisions?

28. Do you know how to manage money efficiently?

29. Do you use the resources of your time, energy, and money on a daily basis in a manner favorable to you moving forward in life?

30. Do you know how to create and implement a budget?

31. Are you openhanded, and generous?

32. Or are you tightfisted?

33. How can being generous help you to accumulate money?

34. How can being tightfisted prevent you from making money?

35. Do you inspire respect or disgust in people with your habits?

36. Do people generally tend to like and respect you?

37. Do people find it easy to do business with you?

38. Do you talk too much? How do you imagine that talking too much could possibly destroy some of your potential business opportunities?

39. Are you educated when it comes to money and finances?

40. Are you broke?

41. If so, why are you broke today?

42. What destructive habits do you have that have led to your financial ruin?

43. Are you a brave, aggressive person with a lot of heart?

44. Are you a timid, cowardly person in need of some heart?

45. Do you make people's lives better when you come in contact with them?

46. Or are you the selfish, manipulative type who never takes into consideration other people's wants and needs only seeing your own?

47. Are you in a destructive relationship that drains your time, energy, and money?

48. If so, are you willing to sacrifice this destructive relationship to succeed?

49. What is the status of your relationship with your family?

50. Will your family support your platinum plan?

51. Do you go out and party all of the **time?**

52. Do you drink too much alcohol'*

53. Do you smoke cigarettes?

54. Do you smoke too many cigarettets? So reflect now on how you can potentially be diagnosed with cancer and kill *your* dreams?

55. Do you use marijuana, cocaine, methamphetamines, heroin, or any other *hard* illegal drug?

56. How can using marijuana, cocaine, methamphetamines, heroin, or any other hard illegal drug potentially destroy all of the success that you may achieve?

57. Do you take control over your sexual desires, or do you let them run wild?

58. Do you have unprotected sex with **unfamiliar,** strange people?

59. How can having unprotected sex with unfamiliar, strange people turn your life upside down and destroy' all of your achievements?

60. Are you in good health? Do you eat a healthy diet?

61. Are you in good enough health to hope to enjoy a million dollars once you have accumulated it?

62. Do you have the appropriate level of focus that you will need to succeed?

63. Do you know what you were born to do?

64. Do you have a purpose in life?

65. Or are you on the way?

66. Do you believe in yourself?

67. Do you believe that you will become e millionaire in this lifetime?

68. Are you ready for success?

69. Or are you afraid of success?

70. What are you willing to do to achieve success in your life and keep it?

These are just a few questions that you should ask yourself to help you become more familiar with your habits and ways which is fundamental to the ***millionaires mind technology*** psychological transformation process. The chief aim of having you answer these questions is to help you to transform your character so that you can become a star business talent. If you successfully have answered any or all of these questions, then your eyes should be opened a little wider and things should be a little clearer in your mind. The key to the exercise that you have just performed is for you to be 100 percent honest with yourself when answering each question. If you cannot bring yourself to be 100 percent honest when answering questions such as these, then you have a serious problem on your hands! If you cannot be honest with yourself, then the problem is you, and you will forever be standing in the way of your success until you open your **mind** and adjust your character. You can never **rise** as high as you can possibly go until you can begin answering questions such as these and be truthful.

I do not expect that you will suddenly change upon reading these questions, but you must decide and make the commitment to yourself that from this point in your life forward, you will strive to be honest about your flaws so that you can transform yourself into the ultimate person that you can be in time. Through making this commitment to yourself, you will open the door to the brightest future available to you. If you always strive for superiority in business and/or soul-searching, you will go far doing things this way. You will see that once you begin to transform your **thinking,** a new world will open up to you! The transformation process will not happen overnight, but the quest starts here! This process is not always easy, so have some patience.

Think. When you set up your **business** operations, you will need to perform certain actions every year continuously. Annually, you will need to perform specific actions such as filing your taxes, taking an inventory of your business, **looking** at your books to measure the profitability of your operation, and periodically check the status of how well your platinum plans are moving along. Just as you will periodically check the status of your platinum plan, you also must periodically check the status of how well your character-transformation process is going. You check the status of your character-transformation process by taking a personal inventory of yourself like this at least once a year. Adopting this practice will help you to get moving forward on the path of becoming a bankable business talent gradually over time. By taking this personal inventory of yourself at least once a year, you can begin to **consciously** see where you are growing in life and measure your progress to start working to increase the areas of your character where you need to become stronger.

Further, you can start to become more consciously aware of where your particular weaknesses and flaws lie so you can then devise a plan of attack for weeding out the weaknesses and flaws out of your character. When you *perform* this annual personal inventory, you should look at exactly how many positive habits that you are **building** up to measure how much closer you are to mastering yourself. Look at doing this annual personal inventory of yourself as basically a way to bring out the best in you!

Equipped with the knowledge of self, you can begin to turn up your shine from the dim glow that you give off **today** and start turning the volume down on the negative things that dull your shine. Gradually in time, you will begin to **shine** as **brightly** as you can!

Filtering this knowledge of self through the new eyes of your **money** consciousness and business mind, now you will recognize that on your rise to the top, a big part of your **climb** to success will be **selling** yourself. When you know **yourself,** you can begin developing yourself into a marketable product, which grows to become a potent brand. Re-creating yourself to become a marketable product and a star entrepreneur in the game is necessary before you can do any business. To transform yourself into a marketable product, you need to know the functions and features of your merchandise, which in this case is you in the form of your talents, skills, strengths, and weaknesses. It is obvious now to see the importance of learning your talents, skills, strengths, and weaknesses. It is one thing to simply desire a **million** dollars. Yet it is quite a different story to actually be worth the amount of money that you seek.

In this world, you will only get paid what you are worth. You must know yourself. If you do not know yourself, then how can you realistically value your worth? When you know yourself, you will be familiar with your specific talents and skills and how to apply these to sell yourself. Applying your talents and **skills** is how you will excel!

Answering the questions in this chapter will help you to begin identifying some of your weaknesses. When you identify your weaknesses, then you can possibly transform these weaknesses of yours into strengths, thus **increasing** your **worth** and marketability. If nothing else, you can neutralize your weaknesses of character rendering them moot or possibly eliminating them all together. As boss, if your character is deficient in certain areas of expertise that you need in your **business,** then to solve this **problem,** you can find and hire smart people who are gifted in the areas that you are weak to work for you.

When you recruit these types of people to join your team, you fill the gaps in your **business** making that state of your affairs whole. In any case, you will need to sell yourself on every level in order to persuade the world that you are worth the amount of riches that you seek. On the whole, if you are to place a price tag on yourself and get **paid** what you believe that you are worth, you must learn to place a **realistic** value on your talents and **skills. Think.** When you go out on **a job interview,** what is the most important thing that you will need? The most important thing that you will need is a good résumé. Your résumé will describe and promote your strong points of character, your talents, and your skills. As an entrepreneur, you will have to build a new résumé showcasing your talents, skills, and **business** track record. This business résumé is a tool that you will use as a selling point in your **business** dealings when pushing your business into new markets and conquering new territories.

As a final note remember, it is not where you are from in the world that will automatically give you an edge in the money game; rather, it is where your mind is at that will help you to rise above and beyond the competition. The *millionaires mind technology* software process is based upon the concept that every form of success that you will ever achieve in your life will start from the **inside** out. First in the process, your success will start on the inside of your mind in the form of your thinking. Then your thoughts will shape the choices and decisions that you make. The choices and decisions that you make will influence your actions. The actions that you take will determine the **quality** and value of your life! Now it is time for you to go into business mode and begin developing some strategies for making some money! Let's go!

$ Money Monetization $

What has the strongest effect upon your emotions? The answer to this question is where you will find your strongest motivation to get money and is also where your deepest satisfaction in life will be found. Your *emotions* are directly related to your motivation. Ask yourself these questions:

- What motivates you to get up every day?
- What drives you in life?
- What are you passionate about?
- What is your strongest desire?
- What do you long for?
- What do you crave?
- Why do you wish to make a billion dollars?

Write out a brief answer to each of these questions. Think long and hard about the answers to each question. _____

Part 2

From Point A to Point Money!

Chapter 5

Boss Mode

This is where the rubber hits the road, and you begin the process of formulating some money-making strategies to get your platinum plans off the ground! But before we get rolling, let's take a *quick* moment of reflection. In part 1 of this book, you were introduced to the **millionaires mind** *technology software* process where you set in motion the *process* of **turning** your vision to look at the world through the *new* eyes of a money-conscious, business-minded individual. With your new eyes in chapter 1, you looked to the road ahead to *analyze* the *current* state of things financial. Then in chapter 2, you went a step further in the process to begin envisioning what your life can become, and at this time, you flooded your imagination with images of your dreams!

Through the mind technology psychological process, your **thinking** should have begun to shift, and your outlook of the world should have advanced allowing you to see within your mind the vast amount of opportunities across America to make your first million using business ownership as your vehicle to reach your financial goals. Further along through the process in chapter 3, you created a platinum plan for making your first million in which you set some goals and began developing some objective strategies for achieving each of the goals that you set. Finally in chapter four, you got your mind **right** by taking an honest introspective look at the areas of your character that you may need to adjust to begin transforming yourself into the ultimate you!

Now in part 2, From Point **A to Point** Money, to fully complete the mind technology psychological transformation process, you will now go into ***boss mode.*** Going into ***boss mode*** is the process of you adopting the outlook of a business person, stepping into the role of the entrepreneur, striking out on a new path of entrepreneurship, and beginning the process of assimilating yourself into the American entrepreneurial *culture*. When you follow the path of business ownership, you will enter into a new dimension of financial possibilities in life that you recently may have thought impossible! In today's world, following the path of entrepreneurship opens the door of opportunity where you can re-create yourself, create your own dream job, restructure your finances, and reset your income! Also, *pursuing* a career as an entrepreneur may not necessarily be as sexy and glamorous as becoming a rock star, a rap star, an actor, a super model, or a professional athlete!

The fact of the matter is that as an entrepreneur, you can potentially make just as much money as the stars if not more! And your shelf life is a lot longer. So now your career as a star entrepreneur starts with the proper mind-set! It does not matter if your dream as an entrepreneur is to rise to become a major player on the local business scene in your **city** or state, or if you dream of **rising** to become a major power player on the national business scene in America. Or perhaps you may see yourself rising to become a business tycoon who owns businesses worldwide and shines in the international business spotlight. Regardless of the scope of your dreams, all of your success will be built upon the foundation of your thinking, your attitude, your approach, and most importantly, your spirit, which takes form in a *strong* faith and belief in yourself.

Think. If you have ever taken the time-out to notice, you will see that the people in life who usually believe they will have it all and believe that they are destined to win are usually the people that end up having it all and winning in life. This is a fact. It is also a fact that people in the world who usually don't believe in themselves and don't expect to win usually end up becoming losers in life. So believing in your self is the foundation. Further, just as you must develop a strong faith and belief in your mind, you must also rid your **mind** of the **belief** that **money** is **a mysterious, elusive** thing that only a chosen few people will touch in life. This belief keeps most people stagnated and stuck. So realize that for you to achieve high levels of success in your life, and to make your mark, you must begin thinking a certain way. As I have stated, your rise to success will begin with the **proper outlook** and **perception** of the world. So from here forward, you will need to drop all of your preconceived notions of money and *how to* accumulate **money** so that you can start over in **life** and move in a new **direction.**

When you change your **thinking,** certain doors of opportunity *will* open up to you in the world that was previously closed. On your million-dollar mission, you must begin moving forward with confidence and be fully focused on where you are headed. You must retire from your past life that has not given you anything of real value and begin striving to achieve success! To make big things happen, you must realize that the world will offer you your chance to shine when you go hard after your dreams and strive for what you desire! Or in simpler words, your financial condition will change from the state that is in today when you change it yourself! And once you begin striving to turn your situation around, then you can have the amounts of money that you strive for.

This concept is very simple, yet it eludes most. The concept is that if you strive to accumulate small amounts of money in your life, then small amounts of money is all that you can expect to gain. And if you strive to accumulate large amounts of money in your life and develop *realistic* plans and strategies to make it happen, then the fruits of your labor will soon come into sight. It is very important that you understand and apply this concept because in order for you to make the big money, you must understand what it takes to make the big money, and without the proper focus, you will almost definitely miss the mark. So understanding the crucial nature of carrying with you the proper mind-set to succeed, we will continue the psychological transformation process of you going into ***boss mode.*** As a boss, you have got to develop a clear picture of the American entrepreneurial culture in your mind and the opportunity that it lays out in front of you to exploit. As boss, to begin developing the proper outlook, you have got to start seeing things in the world as they *truly* are.

To see things as they *truly* are, you will have to become mentally flexible, open- minded, and willing to change and adapt. In your mind, you must constantly zoom in and out to study the big picture of America and the world to help increase your awareness of the economic environment that **surrounds** you today with a goal of developing the proper understanding of our present world financial condition. You also must look back through history to see how we arrived at this point. Lastly, you must try to envision where we are headed in the future. With a clearer vision in your mind of the big picture, you can begin to adapt to the changes in our current economic environment and alter your responses appropriately to the *new economic demands*.

Also, you must *zoom* in to analyze your life. Why? To *mentally* take it apart, to look and observe the *sequence* of *events* that have *culminated* to become your *current financial situation*. Not to make negative **judgments,** but rather, to put ideas together, draw conclusions, and *open* your mind to develop a vision of the new American magazine dream that is spreading across America today. So to *set in motion* the process of you **shaping a dream** in your **mind, rewind** your **mind** back to the time when America was born. This time in history when America was born is the **point** where what we call the American dream was born. The American dream was born with the arrival of the original settlers and all of the *collective* hopes, ambitions, and dreams that they carried in their hearts and **minds.** Then from there, the **American** dream *grew* through all of the collective dreams of each **individual** who have lived the **dream** generation after generation up until now.

Picture all of the *people* through America's history who have come from *humble* beginnings, then dreamed the **dream** and rose to fortune and fame. **Imagine** all of the great challenges that all of these *people* of the *past* dream after dream had to face and overcome to rise! Imagine all of those *people* who used the American free market system to accumulate millions or even billions of dollars from *then until* now! All of these *people's* dreams together **built** the America that surrounds us today. *People's stories* such as these are what the American dream is made of! The dreams of these *people* of our past is also what helped shape the new **American** magazine **dream** we have in America today. So I *suggest* that you draw inspiration from these *people* of our **past** to *develop* within your heart the spirit embodied…

It is called the **American entrepreneurial** *spirit*. The **American** entrepreneurial *spirit* is the spirit of free enterprise. This spirit exists in **America** today! This is the spirit that has made America great! If you are to rise and go the distance in the game of business, you must *capture* this **spirit** and embrace it until it spreads throughout every fiber of your being! It is the spirit of strength, courage, will, force, resilience, and staying power. There is money and opportunity waiting for you in the world when you come to **epitomize** this **spirit.** It is a **spirit** that can**not** and will not be stopped! You must use this spirit to make big things happen! Some excellent examples of entrepreneurs to study who have embodied the American entrepreneurial spirit and are key people who have helped develop the culture are two of the giants of history, John D. Rockefeller and Henry Ford. Or look at today's legends, like Bill Gates, Warren Buffett, Donald Trump, Oprah Winfrey, Russell Simmons, or Steve Forbes, who are all examples of people, in my opinion, who have epitomized this spirit!

In addition to those named above, more **shining** examples of people that you can study who have epitomized the American entrepreneurial spirit and who have also helped develop the culture are entrepreneurial talents such as Mark Zuckerberg, Curtis "50 Cent" Jackson, Jay-Z, Sean "P. Diddy" **Combs,** Kim Kardashian, Ellen Degeneres, or the Olson Twins. These people in my opinion are perfect examples of Americans that show evidence to us all that it is possible to become a millionaire or even a billionaire if you follow your dreams! If you look closely, you will notice that all of these people are American entrepreneurs who have made a pile of money, made a name for themselves, and have achieved their own version of the *new* American magazine dream!

Or if you need more examples of entrepreneurs to gain some inspiration, then you can look to the **millions** of unsung heroes in cities across America who have achieved the American Dream through owning their own businesses today! Studying these types can help demonstrate you what levels of success have been achieved already in America and what is out there to be had. Most of these examples are people who have achieved the American dream through following the path of entrepreneurship. To join the ranks of these types and to assimilate yourself into the culture, you must elevate your sights on doing things as big as you possibly can in your life! To do things as big as you possibly can, you will have to elevate your game and begin playing the game on the major league level. Playing the game on **major** league levels means that you will have to start setting up businesses to compete in the business arena and making money moves like the big boys do in the world of business and trade! It is in the business arena in America that big dreams come true and where the insane fortunes are made!

So now put on your go-getter goggles, so you can start developing some money-**making** strategies! **Think.** What comes to **mind** when you hear the American business arena? The American business arena is the environment where American companies from the largest corporate operations down to the large network of smaller privately owned businesses across America compete. These are the companies that supply the many products and services that we all consume daily.

Usually when we **think** of businesses in the business sector, certain company names come to mind such as 7-Eleven, Coca Cola, Microsoft, Google, Apple, McDonalds, Barnes & Nobles, Sprint, Facebook, Twitter, Hooters, or maybe Office Depot.

Historically, from the largest companies competing across America down to the smaller operations, the entrepreneurial *class* has manufactured the biggest stars in the business arena. Behind most successful businesses across America stands an entrepreneur, who is a leader and a boss, who at one time or another, created the **company. Think.** All of the businesses from the **big corporations** down to smallest operations are different and supply us all with different types of products. Yet all of these businesses are the same in that all of them supply us all with things that we demand. **Think** of the **enormous amount** of **products** that you, your family, your friends, and millions of other *people* across America head out into our cities to purchase each day. We all purchase tons of fast food, designer clothes, toothpaste, vitamins, cell phones, computers, jewelry, cars, flat-screen televisions, Internet service, haircuts, beauty salon services, and whatever else that we desire, want, or need.

The list of companies big and small that supply us with all of the products we demand in the American consumer market goes on and on. Here, we will focus on the smaller network of businesses across America. Why? All companies that have grown to become a success *past* and *present* in America regardless of their size began as small operations! So *depending* on your **financial** situation, it would be *wise* to start **small** and then *gradually* expand and grow your business operations in the future! In America, you can make a fortune with one lucrative idea that is developed into a small business *mixed* with a star strategy to introduce the idea to the American consumer market!

This is where the *big* money is made! This is where you can make your first million! So your focus now is to get in the game by starting up a business of your own!

Today across America from city to city and from sea to shining sea, there is money here for the taking in the private business sector if you find something hot to sell! To make money, you can set up a company around selling anything from culinary creations, to cars, clothes, computers, condoms on up to condominiums! So do not let **starting-up** and running businesses worry or intimidate you. You can do it! As an entrepreneur, you can win by using your **money** consciousness to locate cash sources that are available to you and use your business mind to formulate strategies to get the money! In the role of an entrepreneur, the first order of **business** for you will be for you to locate a business venture for you to invest in and then set up your first company:

> ➡ Generate a solid stream or streams of Income!
>
> ➡ **Turn** some profits!
>
> ➡ Fatten your pockets and bank accounts!
>
> ➡ And stack up some green dollars to make you a million!

From this **point** forward, you must break **out** on a new path to begin investing in yourself, investing in your plans, and investing your dreams. To make your dreams real, you must start looking into the world for opportunities to make some money in business. Today in America, there is a demand for many new products and services that you can discover to sell. If you can possibly catch a *current,* or even *anticipated* hot new product or service to **build** a business around, then that can possibly be a gold mine that you can **exploit.** For instance, all of the **economic** evils that we see in the *news* today can be a signal pointing you in the right direction of what you can possibly sell.

Whether our economy is in the midst of a boom or bust cycle, regardless of the financial weather, anything is possible in the American free market business arena! You can set up a business around almost anything these days! It is your time now because the chosen ones choose themselves! But you have got to be in it to win it! The fact that you have your platinum plans in hand puts you a step ahead of the game. But a lot goes with that. Creating your **platinum** plan is only half of the battle. After that, it is the effective execution of your platinum plan that will win you the war! Looking at making your **first million** as you're fighting your own economic war will give you an edge. Yes, my friend, **making** your first million dollars perhaps may be the biggest war that you will ever fight! And winning this war for you is a matter of financial life or death! So **suit** up and prepare to do battle! In preparation, know **thy** enemy is an age-old warfare strategy that many great generals have **utilized** before heading into battle.

Before heading into battle, you must begin to recognize and know your enemy. In the world of business and trade as well as in life in general, your enemy is poverty, lack, **being broke,** and all that goes along with that. Upon **identifying** this enemy, you must go on the attack and wage war! With your enemy in your scope, you must devise some strategies to fight this enemy in any form that it may take. Recognize that this enemy takes the form of anything in your life that may stand in the way of you achieving your dreams! With that in mind, you must now go into your war room. And with your eyes on the long-term objectives of your platinum plan, you must begin formulating your strategies to conquer the everyday financial battles that you will face on the road ahead while using each battle as a footstep in your overall strategy to win the war!

So with the outlook of a modern-day conqueror, you must begin devising your plan of attack! Imagine each business opportunity that you set your sites on is an opportunity to conquer new territory and **plant** your flag in new soil! This is the American way! Get in to it! Now to help you *set in motion,* the process of building your first business. In the following *chapters,* I will introduce you to the millionaires mind technology *software* business-building model. This is a complete model for building businesses in a profit portfolio. It's designed to assist you in building a *winning* company to enter the competition that is now taking place in the American business arena! The business-building model will demonstrate:

> 1. Build winning business blueprints!
>
> 2. Finance your business operation.
>
> 3. Begin building your first business.
>
> 4. Manage **your** profit **portfolio.**
>
> 5. Evolve your *platinum plan!*

This business-building model that I will offer you here is a model of business building in American you can clone as a **blueprint** for your rise! In it, I will *describe* a broad overview of the technical business knowledge that you will need to gain to get moving in the **right** direction toward your success! This process will show you *how to* bring a business idea out of your mind and then *develop* it into a fully functional business. (The first business that you build will be *very* important because the profits that it potentially generates will help you to achieve the goals in your platinum plan.)

Now that you have a clear **vision** of where you are headed and are motivated to take the necessary actions to make it happen, then everything else will be born from your hustle. Starting from where you are financially, you must begin discovering creative ways to turn your situation around. You must be determined to achieve your dreams to the point that you will not let **nothing** or no one stand in your way! The rapper 50 Cent named his breakout CD that made him rich, *Get Rich or Die Trying*! This statement pretty much sums up the attitude you should **adopt** as you step into becoming a star entrepreneur. You must internalize and mentally absorb this concept until you fully understand this statement's significance and the power it holds. Then make the declaration that you will get rich or die trying yourself! This does not mean that you will place yourself in any **harmful** situations to **accumulate** riches.

    Rather, it means that you will have an iron will to succeed and an unshakable drive and determination to get rich standing tall in the face of any and all obstacles that may stand in your way on the road ahead. Know that anyone who has ever accumulated a great fortune in this world had to face many obstacles and great challenges before everything came together. And although there are exceptions to every rule, you are no different from the others. So be prepared to face many obstacles and heavy opposition to your platinum plan. *Many people in your life may not readily come to believe in you and what you are planning to do. But you **believing** in the creator and **believing** in yourself will be enough!* But regardless of who supports you, make it up in your mind right now that you will do whatever it takes to make it happen. And under absolutely no circumstances will you ever quit, or give up! Ready. Set. Let's go!

Chapter 6
Build Winning Business Blueprints

On the road **ahead** as you step into the role of entrepreneur, you will have your work cut out for you. The entrepreneurial way of life is not cut out for everyone. As they say, many are called, but the chosen are few. But fortunately for you, if you have what it takes on this playing field, the chosen ones choose themselves! Competing in the American business **arena,** there is always an immense ocean of **opportunity** waiting for anyone who is bold enough to go for it! When you yourself make the choice to pursue a career in the world of business and trade, then this ocean of immense **opportunities** to accumulate a **fortune** will open up to you! This is very true. If you are bold enough to go for it, then specifically, you can seize the opportunities that exist in the business arena by getting your hands on a hot product or service that you can **build** a business around to generate yourself some revenues and turn some profits!

Now to get the wheels rolling, you will have to map out your course! But before moving forward, I must make it clear that while the opportunity for you to make a million dollars is out there waiting for you, on the flip side of that coin, you must also *realize* that there is no guarantee that you will make a million dollars. Or that you will even make one green dollar. Why? Because there are never any guarantees in life. I say this because it is important that you have a well-rounded perspective of the challenge that you will face ahead first so that you can fully prepare to rise to face the challenge!

As an entrepreneur, it is very important that you understand that making a million dollars will not be an easy task to undertake, but it is possible. If it was easy to go out and make a million dollars, then everyone would be millionaires today. Right? With that said, the fact is that in America and the world, the opportunity to make money in business will always be here. Because from now until the end of time, people will always be hungry for a new product or service to buy that is produced to satisfy our many desires, wants, needs, and problems! Setting up businesses around satisfying any of these many desires, wants, needs, or problems is where the big money is to be made!

Specifically, the process of creating businesses and controlling the money that flows through these businesses is the financial technique that you must apply to make your first million. This is the entrepreneurial way. As an entrepreneur, you must become an innovator of business enterprise who recognizes business opportunities where others do **not** and then seize these opportunities by **building** businesses around these **opportunities** that you discover.

Specifically, you must pull together the necessary factors of production to supply the demand. This process describes the basics of doing business. So if you have a mind for business, the money is out there. Now once you know what it will take to make it happen, then from that point forward, your immediate focus should be to position yourself to start making some cash by you setting up your very first business. All it takes today to make a million is for you to find one *hot new* product or service that you can build a business around! To discover a product or service to build lucrative business around, you will have to make use of your money consciousness and business mind.

From the beginning, recognize that doing business is not all about chasing a quick dollar; rather, to be successful in the business arena, you must think long term, dig your heels in, and be prepared to be in it for the long haul. This is important to understand because success in business doesn't come over night. To succeed, you must first lay a solid foundation and then put in the necessary work to be a success! In business, once you locate something hot to sell and set up a fully functioning company around your product or service, then you won't have to chase a dollar rather once you are in position you can sit back and let the money come to you! So here we are! You have platinum plans and magazine dreams that you have to set in *motion* ASAP, but where do you start? This is where you psychologically go into business attack mode and begin formulating your plans and strategies to begin transforming your life from rags to riches! From day one, you must get into the **habit** of thinking strategically.

In **business** as in war, you do not want to enter either without prior proper planning or without adequate funding. Once again, remember that having created your platinum plan is only half the battle. After that, the successful execution of your plan is the focus. You can create the most intelligent plans in the world, but without the appropriate ways and means to put your plans in full effect, then your plans are worthless. The appropriate ways and means that you will need to put your **plans** in full effect is the specific money-generating plans and strategies that you must craft to accomplish your million-dollar goal and the money that you raise to set your plans and strategies into motion. Locating the appropriate ways and means to put your platinum plans in full effect should command your full attention now.

At this point, even if you have no idea how you will get your hands on the money that you will need to finance your plans, you will have to get yourself fully prepared first to help increase your chances of success. Do not worry because once you reach a state of full preparation where there is a will, there is a way. If you can't find a way, then you will make one! Because there is always money and resources out there available to you in the world, but you must seek them out and find them! Now to begin the process of you locating the appropriate ways and means to put your platinum plans in full effect at this moment, *zoom* your mind into focus on your million-dollar goal. In your mind's eye, imagine where you are today financially and from there, envision yourself rising to achieve your dreams. Imagine yourself achieving the goals in your platinum plan in **vivid** detail. Specifically **imagine** what **practical steps** you will need to take to reach millionaire status. Starting here, you will map out your course and begin the process of devising your plans and strategies to begin transforming your life from rags to riches!

To set **in motion** the process, take the time-out now to **think** forward and visualize how you will achieve your **dream** in **vivid** detail. **Fast forward** your **thoughts** to **think** about what role that you will play in the world twenty years from now. Where do you see yourself financially twenty years from now? See all of the people, places, and things that you **imagine** that will surround you at that time. Imagine what your life can potentially become. Now rewind your mind back ten years from that point. Where do you see yourself financially ten years from now? Now rewind your mind back five years from that point. Where do you see yourself financially five years from now? How will you get there? What steps must you begin to take today to get there?

Now imagine where you will be two years from today financially. Where do you see yourself financially two years from now? Now where do you see yourself financially one year from now? Starting with a vision of your immediate future, you must begin to craft some practical plans with a focus on you using what you have in the form of money and resources to get what you want out of life. In your mind's, eye see your platinum plan as your master hustle plan that will guide you and give your life direction. You must take the time-out to begin **thinking** hard and **imagining** creative ways to use all of the knowledge and information that you have gathered up and developed in the previous chapters as a guide to begin formulating your short-term plans and strategies to turn your life around and get on track to begin moving toward achieving the goals in your platinum plan. With the goals of your **platinum** plan in your mind mixed with the vision of your dreams, you must begin looking at your current financial situation, your income, your overhead cost of living, your debt, and your available cash to gain a realistic perspective of where you are.

Upon seeing things as they truly are, in order to lay the proper foundation, you will need to adjust the objective strategies that you have developed in your platinum plan to reflect your current financial position. Once you have adjusted the objective strategies that you have developed in your platinum plan to reflect your current financial position, from there your immediate plans and strategies to get things off the ground should blossom. Using your platinum plan as your solid base of plans, begin the process of formulating your immediate plans and strategies remembering that success moves in cycles. You must start from the bottom and **gradually** move to the top.

With your mind *focused* on formulating your grand strategy to rise and become a major player in the business game, first you must focus on locating some lower-level hustles to begin touching some money you can play with! The upward motion of your plans to rise from the ground up should then follow the *logic* of what I have labeled the money accumulation gradation process. The money accumulation gradation logic states that in order for you to make your **first million,** you first must discover an *opportunity* you can invest in to make your first hundred thousand dollars. And to make your first hundred grand, you first must locate a hustle that can make you some thousands. And in order for you to make some thousands, you first must find a way to make some hundreds. And to make some **hundreds,** you *need* one profitable idea to make your first green dollar! So it's safe to say that your rise will begin with solid ideas.

From this point forward, remember that all forms of success will start in your mind in the form of ideas. In the role of entrepreneur, you will be in charge of locating lucrative business ideas to invest in. To help shape your business mind, you must become aware that on the *most basic level,* all businesses in the world start in the form of ideas. Ideas grow to become demand. Demand becomes *hot* products and services. Then products and services become fully **functional** businesses. Now this brings us to the business-**building** model where I will show you how to **build** winning business blueprints! ***Phase 1.*** This phase, **build winning** business blueprints, will illustrate the process of generating *hot* business ideas that can be used to begin building businesses. Here, we will begin the process of helping you to discover at least one *hot* product or service that you can **build** the first business in your profit portfolio around.

Ideas for new businesses can **originate** from many different sources. In their rawest form, good businesses ideas are born from a strong desire, want, need, or problem that a group of people in the world share. Imagine that when people across America and the world head out into the world with their purses and pocketbooks in hand to purchase any **product** or service from any business, at that time, they are being motivated and driven to satisfy one of their desires, wants, needs, or problems when they buy whatever they are purchasing.

➡ Desires are things that we long and crave for.

➡ Wants are the stuff that we buy but do not really need to survive.

➡ Needs are the very things that we buy that are directly related to our survival. Such as food, **clothing, and** shelter.

➡ Problems are the evils that touch our lives that we pay other people in the world to solve and eliminate.

Picture in your mind ideas that represent a strong desire, want, need, or problem that a community of people may share in your city or wherever you plan to do business.

Thinking of how you can create a product or service that satisfies a strong desire, want, need, or problem that a community of people may share in your city can help you discover a business idea that you can possibly build your first business around.

See in your **mind's** eye that every city across America and the world has within its borders communities of people that all share collective sets of desires, wants, needs, and problems. As an entrepreneur, finding creative ways to satisfy any of these collective sets of desires, wants, needs, or problems that a group of people may share is how you locate lucrative business opportunities for you to invest in and pursue. So once again, keep in mind that ideas become products and services:

> ➡ Products are tangible, material things that businesses produce that we can walk away with in our hands upon **purchase.**
>
> ➡ Services are things that businesses produce through the efforts of physical labor or through the work of machines and or other equipment.

So when putting on your *go-getter goggles* to look into your world for a lucrative business opportunity to build a business around, if you happen to discover a collective set of desires, wants, needs, or problems that a specific group of people may share in your city, or in any city that you may be interested to do business in, or on the Internet, then there is a possibly where your opportunity to build your first business around may be waiting. Opportunities are everywhere. You just have to put your ear to the ground and do your **homework! Imagine** that all of the **products** or services that are currently being offered for sell through businesses in your **city,** or in other cities across the **world,** or on the Internet first started in the form of an idea. These ideas, if developed into products and services with a strong demand, then become lucrative businesses.

So starting here, you will need to find at least one idea to **build** the first business in your **profit portfolio** around. At this moment, take the time-out to picture what specific business idea that you could possibly **build** your first business around? Ideas for new businesses can originate from many different sources:

1. You can think of a brand-new idea that you discover and develop from scratch.

2. You can piggyback off of someone else's idea by **building upon** their idea with your **creativity** and **ingenuity** and make their idea better.

3. Or you could possibly work **together** with **a creative person** using their **mind** to generate an idea for yourself. Together, you can carve up the profits with them after you develop their **idea** and make it available to the **market.**

Now when moving through the process of locating a profitable business idea to invest in, if you happen to choose any of the methods spelled out above to generate your idea, do not worry because anyway, what you choose is cool. The reality is that it does not really matter from whose mind a lucrative business idea originates as long as it ends up making you some money! Right? Always keeping the highest ethical standards if you lack good **ideas,** then you can *recruit* intelligent people to work for you and make their ideas your own. Just because you are not a creative thinker does not mean that you will have to stop there. The goal is for you to get into the game and make some money! You must find the method for generating ideas that suits your style of doing business.

Now you must decide in what city or forum that you will set up your first business. You can **set up** your first business in your **city;** or if you ascertain that there is big money flowing in someone else's city, then if you like, you can set up a business there; or you can set up a business on the Internet. Whatever city or setting that your **financial** ambitions may lead you in order for you to discover a solid business idea to invest in, turn your vision to imagine all of the people that inhabit that city or forum to your focus. And through the eyes of your money consciousness and business mind, study these people with an eye looking to uncover a product or service that represents a strong desire, want, need, or problem that this group shares together in their lives. The stronger the desire, want, need, or problem that this group of people may share, the stronger the demand for whatever that you will be **offering** these people for sell.

> ➡ Demand is the amount of a product or service that people are ready and able to buy at a given time at a certain place.

Business is all about supply and demand. The idea is the foundation of the operation. So if the demand for the product or service is weak, then the operation will be weak.

And if the demand for the product or service is strong, then the operation will be strong. It is very important that you always build businesses around a strong demand. As a rule, never commit any of your time, energy, or money to building a business around a product or service where no true demand exists. In my opinion, most businesses fail because people build businesses around a product or service where no true demand existed. Or they could not appropriately supply the demand that existed.

The best-laid business plans in the world will fail if there is no real demand for the product or service that is being put on the market. So how do you find something hot to sell that has a strong demand? In this world, everything is based on perception. So in order for you to find something hot to sell that has a strong demand, you must understand people and perceptions. Business is all about producing and supplying products and services that satisfy a desire, want, need, or problem in real, everyday, flesh-and-blood people. All people in the world have their own set of values, feelings, beliefs, and unique perceptions of themselves and the world around them. With that in mind, to help you locate an idea that you can possibly **build** your first **business** around, you will now need to turn your vision and **shift** your perspective to imagine the world through the eyes of the people that you will target to be your customers.

To locate something hot to offer these people for sell, you have got to psychologically step into their skin, walk in their shoes, and look at the world through their eyes. As you look at the world through their eyes, then ask yourself:

> ➡ What do these people desire?
>
> ➡ What do they want?
>
> ➡ What do these people need?
>
> ➡ **Or** what **problem of theirs could I possibly** solve?

Your goal is to sell something that is in demand and thinking like your target customers is your secret weapon. This will put you in a strong position to do business from.

Imagine every morning that the **sun rises** all across America, there are companies opening their doors to do business with the world through supplying **products** and services that we all demand. On a daily basis in this arena, some of the businesses that are competing are winning, some are losing, and others are in the middle. To hit the ground running, you will have to get in where you fit in and start making some power plays by setting up a business around selling something hot with a strong demand! All it will take is one good idea to get you started! As an extra incentive, when you enter the game, it does not really matter what you start off selling as long it is legal and can generate you some profits! Now in whatever city that you are located in the world, I would *suggest* that you set in motion your campaign to takeover and begin rising in the game through competing in a market in your city. Develop your short-range business plans around selling a *product* or *service* in your section that will help you get on your feet, cut out your niche, establish your territory, and solidify yourself a top spot to eat.

Okay. Right now, you will have to make a choice. At this point in the process, you should have a general idea of an idea that you will build your first business around. Now to draw up a set of winning business blueprints for yourself, first you must select an idea that you can develop into a product or service with a strong demand. Then once you have selected an idea, you will have to create a detailed plan of action to get your idea out of your mind and into the marketplace! This detailed plan of action should describe your market, your target customers, and your competition. Additionally, your plan should spell out how you will develop your product or service, packaging design, your price, and how you will distribute your products or services to your clientele.

Take as much time as you need to carefully think things through and select your idea. Visualize your idea in your mind. Ask yourself what product or service idea could I possibly create a successful business around? Then stop and write out a description of your product or service idea and why you believe that your idea will provide you with a lucrative business opportunity. Also write out how you plan to develop your product or service idea into a business. My product or service idea:

Now describe your market. A market is anywhere in your city, in the world, or on the Internet that brings together businesses that are supplying products or services with customers who are willing to buy these products or services. My market:

_____
_____
_____
_____
_____
_____
_____
_____
_____
_____
_____
_____
_____
_____
_____
_____
_____
_____
_____
_____
_____
_____
_____
_____
_____
_____
_____
_____
_____

Now write out a brief psychological description of your target customer archetype. The more detailed the description of your target customer that you can build up, the better. Your psychological description can include their likes, their dislike, their desires, wants, needs, or problems. It can describe their income levels, their spending power, spending habits, what motivates them to spend money, their perceptions of themselves, and their perceptions of the world around them. It can describe their beliefs, values, culture, and religion. My target customer archetype description:

_____
_____
_____
_____
_____
_____
_____
_____
_____
_____
_____
_____
_____
_____
_____
_____
_____
_____
_____
_____
_____
_____
_____
_____

Then you will have to do your homework and learn who will be offering the same product or service in your market. This is your competition. **Describe** your competition. Then describe your relationship with them. (You can plan to eliminate the competition, neutralize their effectiveness in the market, or strategically align yourself with them to solidify your market position.) My competition:

_____
_____
_____
_____
_____
_____
_____
_____
_____
_____
_____
_____
_____
_____
_____
_____
_____
_____
_____
_____
_____
_____
_____
_____
_____
_____
_____

Now once you have completed the process of **drawing up** a written description of your target market, a psychological description of your target customer, and a description of your competition, then after that, you must focus on product or service development. The product development process begins with the idea that you have chosen. While you may have possibly selected an excellent idea, you still must go further to research and test your ideas with potential customers to determine if a demand exist. This is an extremely **important** step in the process. Why? Before you **commit** any of your time, energy, or money on **building** any business you should always do your homework first to ascertain if a true demand exists for the product or service in the city or forum in which you plan to do business.

During this process you will:

1. Generate a new product or service idea.

2. Create a product or service prototype and find potential customers to test it and offer you feedback.

3. Adjust your product or service in response to your potential customer's ideas.

4. Construct your budget for producing the product or service and your plan to bring your product or service to the market.

5. Bring together the factors of production to supply the demand. (facilities, equipment, and staff for manufacturing your product or service).

Once you have completed this process, then you will have to select a brand name for your product or service, design the packaging for what you are selling, set your prices, and finally, you will have to outline your distribution plan and strategy.

When selecting the brand name for your product or service, you should choose a name that characterizes what you are selling in the most professional way possible. As you generate a name, keep in mind that each product or service line that you introduce in any of your businesses must be branded. Branding, as it relates to business, is the process of molding and shaping the perceptions of your product or service lines in the minds of your **customers.** You must establish your branding process from day one.

The goal of this process is to set each of your product or service lines apart from the other products or services in the market. This will allow each of your products or services to establish their own name, identity, and market position. Now you must choose a name. I *suggest* that you choose an attractive name that you can brand heavily. The brand name of my product or service:

➡ Brand name:_____

Upon choosing a name for your product or service, you will then have to design how it will be packaged. Packaging is the style of the wrapping, the covering, or the casing of your product or service. In this context, image is everything! People pay money for what appeals to their five senses. If it looks good, and they find it to be attractive, they will buy it! If it tastes good, they will buy it! If it smells good, they may buy it! If it sounds good, they will buy it! If it feels good, it's sold! Make your product or service as seductive as possible! Study other similar products and services that are on the market to get a feel for how the competition is packaging their goods and services. **Study** the market then develop packaging that makes your product or service shine!

Now set your prices. Here, you must establish the amount of money that you will charge your customers in exchange for the product or service that you are offering and the specific method of payment that you will accept. While there are a many factors in every market that will influence the pricing of certain products or services, keep in mind that pricing is not an exact science. Overall, all of your business transactions should be aimed at **making** a profit. Your profit margin then will be directly related to the prices that you charge. So look at pricing as a juggling act between satisfying your customers and satisfying your pockets. Your price-setting goals:

1. To cover the cost of doing business and also turn a profit.

2. Set prices that your customers will perceive as a superior deal.

3. Never set your prices too high or too low. Why? This will position you at a competitive disadvantage in your market.

Your three **strategic pricing objectives**:

1. Capitalize on your **profits.** If you have a short supply of a **product** or service that is in high demand, then increase your prices to make a higher profit.

2. Increases your sales volume. If you have a large supply of a product or service for sale and you are facing heavy competition, then lower your prices to increase sales.

3. Maintain your image. Your prices should support the image that you are shaping in the minds of your customers through the branding process.

Now you will have to set the price(s) that you will charge your customers in exchange for the **product** or service that you will be **offering** and spell **out** in detail the method of payment that you will accept. (You can accept cash, check, credit card, or whatever method that you choose. You're the boss!) I will charge:

The **price** I will **charge** for my **product** or **service**: $_____

My method of payment:

_____

_____

Now at last, you must create a plan describing how you will distribute your products or services to your market in a cost-effective manner. As the boss, you will have to decide at what location your product or service will be sold and what means of shipping your company will utilize. Deciding how you will distribute your products or services to your customers may be one of the greatest challenges that you will face as a business owner. To begin mapping out your distribution plan, think through the path that your product or service will take from your company's production location to where your customers will conduct business with you. Today with the Internet at your disposal and other technology, you can do business on a global level. (Also nowadays through the services of companies like Amazon, FedEx and UPS, you can distribute your products all over the world by **land, air,** or sea in a very cost-effective manner.)

THE ART OF MAKING MONEY

I suggest that you employ the services of companies such as those named above to make the distribution process for yourself easier. Also, to give yourself a competitive advantage in the game, you must make effective use of computers and other business technology, which will allow you to be more productive and work more efficiently. Now draw up a written description of your distribution plan! My distribution plan:

Now at this point, you should have selected a product or service that you will **build** your first business around. But before we conclude this *phase,* keep in mind that as you *move* through the product development stage, your chief task as an entrepreneur is to *listen* closely to your market to ascertain the desires, wants, needs, and problems this group collectively shares that is currently going unsatisfied and to begin designing products and services that satisfy these desires, wants, needs, and problems in your target markets. Further, in the role of entrepreneur, your chief task is to develop products to be introduced to your markets that these groups of people actually want and not the products that you want to sell! So as an entrepreneur, you must be relentless in this pursuit of finding new *unsatisfied* wants, needs, desires, and problems of your target customers and creating *new* products to exploit the **opportunity!** When *seeking* to make your **first million** your success will *rest upon* how effectively you *develop* new products to satisfy your customer's collective appetites.

Now once you have completed the process of creating a set of **winning** business blueprints, you then must *turn* your *vision* to focus on *creating* a plan of action to raise the money to finance your business operation! This is a problem that can become a *major* stumbling block that will *surface* on the road ahead. This problem is usually one of the biggest challenges in business building that *you will face*. So in the chapter that follows, you will focus on tackling this problem. Do not be discouraged. Why? *When there is a will, there is a way!* So at this moment, you will need to activate your money consciousness and *zoom* in to focus configuring out the answer to the question of how will you raise the cash to finance your business operation? Ready. Set! Let's go!

Chapter 7

Finance Your Business Operation

So you have decided upon a business opportunity to pursue. Congratulations! Now let's zoom in to focus on solving the problem of how you plan to raise the necessary funds to finance your business operation. ***Phase 2.*** Selecting the course of action that you will follow to raise your *start-up* cash may be one of the *greatest obstacles* that you will have *to face* and *overcome* on the road ahead. In this chapter, we will look into the process of *how to* **formulate** a tactical **game plan** to tackle this **money** problem.

As with every aspect of the ***millionaires mind technology software*** process, you will have to approach this with an **open mind,** be flexible, and willing to **adapt** in order to find creative methods for capitalizing upon any set *of favorable circumstances* or *financial conditions* that may take *shape* in your life. This may *serve* as a practical means for you to possibly achieve your **platinum** plans, **goals,** and **objective** strategies.

At this point with the creation of your platinum plan, you should currently have a huge, **strategic** vision of where you want your life to go financially. And further through having developed a set of winning business blueprints, you should now have a potential vehicle that can be used as a practical means for reaching your million-dollar dream destination! Now all you are lacking is the fuel to get moving! The fuel in this instance is your businesses start-up cash! And as the saying goes, it takes money to make money! Without any money, your platinum plan will be dead in the water.

Now in a perfect world, once you have reached the point where you have **created** your **platinum plan,** ideally at that time, the money that you need to bring your plans to life will be readily available. But more times than not, this will not be the case in real life. At this moment, take the time-out to think and ask your self, "Where will I get the **money** to **finance** my **business?**" Upon answering this question, if at that time you realize that you do not immediately have access to the money that you will need in your checking accounts, in your nest egg savings, in a shoe box, or somewhere else; or if you do not have family, friends, or associates with deep pockets that will get behind you and put the money up to finance your **business;** or if you cannot readily call to mind any other source that you can think of to supply you with a lump sum of money that you can invest in your **business** idea, then you will have to hustle and strive to raise the **money** yourself. Yeah, I said **hustle** to get it yourself. **Hustling** is the **American** way!

Now when we **think** of the word hustler and **hustling,** usually we will call to mind the image of some two-bit, sleazy individual with a cigarette dangling from their lips while running one illegal operation or another. Yet in the real-world money game, this is not the case. The real hustlers of the world are **entrepreneurs, managers,** and other career people grinding each day for a salary or a paycheck just like you and me! Now as a rule, when on your **money-motivated mission** never use fraud, deception, or any illegal means to accumulate money. If for any reason you do choose to engage in fraud, deception, or any illegal **business,** then be warned that you may win for a time, but eventually things will come to the light. And you will be **penalized,** kicked out the game, and **lose.** So don't do it! Now let's get your **brain** in the **game** and help you to start **thinking** like a **hustler.**

At this moment, put on your hustler's hat to envision and pose to yourself this question. What specific hustle could you possibly use to raise enough money to finance your **business operation?** The **process** set forth in this chapter will help you to begin *thinking* like a hustler in order for you to figure out a specific hustle you can use to raise your businesses start-up cash. To begin the process of *shaping* your **hustler's** *perspective,* you will need to follow a five-step *process.* This five-step *process:*

➡ 1. Asses **your** current financial **position.**

➡ 2. Determine your business operations financial needs.

➡ 3. Set short-term financial goal to hustle-up cash.

➡ **4. Locate a cash source to supply your financial needs.**

➡ **5. Unleash your hustle!**

NOTE—this five-step process should be viewed as a bridge to help connect your reality with your dreams! Learning this five-step process is essential because even if you create the greatest plans in the world without a **practical** means for raising the cash to finance your **business** operation, the platinum plan you created will be like a car without an engine, a bird without wings, or our *new world* without the Internet! With this first problem, you will learn the process of hustling skillfully. On the road ahead in the capacity of a boss **hustling** entrepreneur, you will need to continually apply this five-step process from **point** A to **point money!** Here, I will set forth some **guiding** steps for you to follow, but you yourself must find the method that fits your style of doing business. As a suggestion, take the time-out presently think, reflect, and absorb the process.

1. ASSESS YOUR CURRENT FINANCIAL POSITION

Now as a **hustler,** you should always be aware of what you are worth in the **form** of dollars and cents at any given moment of the day. So starting now, you must place a price tag on yourself. Placing a price tag on yourself is the act of you going through the process of evaluating and calculating your current net worth. Your net worth is calculated through weighing on a scale what you own in the form of assets against what you owe in the form of **liabilities.** Assets in simple words are all of the things that you own that have value. Your assets can include things such as **liquid** assets in the **form** of cash on hand or money in your **checking** and savings accounts, or **money** that people owe you or tax refund money you will have due this tax season. Assets can also come in the form of the cash value of your life insurance, certificates, **bonds,** stocks, mutual **fund** shares, or any **precious** metals that you possess. Your fixed assets can include the value of your car, your home, your **furniture,** your jewelry, and other personal property that has value. Deferred assets can consist of things such as a 401(k) plan, an **IRA,** or any other retirement plan. Make a list of all of your assets and add them up.

Liabilities in simple words are financial burdens that you carry in the form of **debt. Liabilities** are things such as charge accounts, taxes due, credit card debt, student loans, your current bills due, or any other outstanding lines of credit. Also, liabilities are any car loans, mortgage loans, personal loans, or any other **forms** of debt that you owe. Make a list of all of your liabilities and add them up. Once you know the sum total of your assets and the **total** of all of your **liabilities,** then you must do some **money mathematics.**

When you subtract what you owe in the form of **liabilities** from what you own in assets, then the remaining number will represent your net worth. Once you have successfully calculated your current net worth, then after that, you then must go further to assess the cash flowing in and out of your life. Your cash flow is calculated by adding up all of your current income streams. Income streams can consist of a salary, or other wages from working that you plan to collect. Add up all of the money that you have coming in each month. Then you have to add up all of the expenditures that represent your monthly overhead. Your monthly overhead is your bills and other **expenses** that you have to pay out each month. Your overhead expenditures can include expenses such as food, rent, utilities, automobile payments, gas, entertainment, clothes shopping, debt payments, and other miscellaneous expenses. Understanding your **net worth,** how much income that you have incoming as well as what you are spending will help you to begin the **process** of **shaping** your **hustler's perspective.**

Constant awareness of these **numbers** and the balancing of these **numbers** in your head will help to keep your mind focused on the score board and will serve as ruler to measure how far you will need to travel from here to the point where you achieve your **platinum** plans goals! Once you do the assessment of your current net worth and your cash flow, then you will have reached a major milestone on your **money-motivated mission!** It is important that you perform these steps because you cannot know where you are going if you do not first know where you are at or where you have been. You must create a clear vision in your mind of your financial past, present, and future before you can establish a **strong** hustle. Take your time and complete this step before **moving forward.**

2. DETERMINE YOUR BUSINESS OPERATIONS FINANCIAL NEEDS

To begin formulating a tactical game plan to raise the money to finance your business operation, you will need to determine your specific business needs. One word to learn as a hustler is research. As boss, you will need to follow a line of **investigation** to learn your business and industry inside and out. Until you have **money** to hire people to do your research, this is your job. There are many different methods that you can use to perform your research, but some ways can be more effective than others. Remember that we live in the information age and that the Internet places a world of information at your fingertips. The Internet is a great starting point to begin your research. Websites such as Google, Bing, and Yahoo! just to name a few are vast sources to supply you with your business research information. You can also make use of libraries, colleges, or business mentors to supply you with information to make **decisions** for your business. So how do you determine your business needs?

Each business and industry will have its specific methods and practices for gathering research information. The method that you employ to gather **information** for your specific operation will be dictated by what particular business that you plan to create.

Just as each individual human being has their own individual personality and needs, each business will have its own unique needs. There are no hard rules for gathering information in business due to the uniqueness of each business. But there are some general guidelines that you can follow to specifically define what your **business** will need. Remember that this is only a starting point to begin your exploration.

You have got to ask the right questions to begin the research process. The focus of the research-gathering task is to unearth information to aid in making your **business** decisions. In this instance, you will need to perform an investigation:

➡ How much money must you raise in order to adequately finance your business operation?

Ascertaining precisely how much money you will need to raise in order to finance your business operation will help you to get started off on the right foot. Generally, your business start-up cost will consist of three components:

➡ Stack A: Stack A will cover all of your fixed and variable cost that you will have to shell out for you to set up your business. Your cost can include things such as business licenses, permits, your lease, furniture, computers, equipment, phones, technology, inventory, research, development, marketing, human resources, and all other cost to set up your business.

➡ Stack B: Stack B will cover the amount of cash that you will have to shell out to keep your business up and running from day one and until you can recoup your initial investment, make a profit, and then get your business well into the black.

➡ Stack C: Stack C will serve as your cash cushion strategically calculated to cover any unforeseen business cost, emergencies, and as a reserve to provide seed money for any *new* business opportunities that may present themselves.

Although every **business** has its own unique set of needs, these three components should help serve as general guidelines to help direct the focus of your research activities. The goal here is for you to learn how much that it will cost for you to bankroll your specific type of business. You must gain the knowledge of your business needs.

The focus of your research is to first determine how much money that you will need to raise in order to set your business operation up. Your businesses start up needs will cover your production cost, marketing cost, and the cost of your human resources. To determine your businesses specific needs, ask and answer the following questions:

➡ How big of a market exist for my businesses product?

➡ How many people in my market can I reasonably attract and serve?

➡ How big of a product inventory will I need to build up?

➡ What **production facilities** will be required to produce my **product?**

➡ How much will it cost to set up my production facilities?

➡ What resources are needed to create my product, and how much will the resources cost to produce enough products to supply my market?

➡ How will I supply my production facilities with the natural resources, component **parts,** and other needed materials to **produce** my **product?**

➡ Who will be my suppliers, and how will I contract to compensate them?

➡ What will be my **marketing** strategy?

➡ How will I **distribute** my **products** to my target market?

➡ How much will it cost me to distribute my products to my target market?

➡ How will I promote my products to my target market?

➡ How will I identify and communicate with my target market audience?

➡ How much will it cost me to promote my **products** to my target market?

➡ What human resources will be needed to help run my business?

➡ Will I pay my employees a salary, hourly wages, a commission, or a combination of these compensation structures?

➡ How much will it cost me to hire and train my staff?

➡ How much will it cost me to bankroll my payroll?

These questions will help you to begin clarifying your business needs and help you to determine how much money you will need to raise in order to finance your business.

3. SET SHORT-TERM FINANCIAL GOAL TO HUSTLE UP CASH

Take the time-out right now in this moment to perform a money meditation. The focus of this money meditation is for you to open your mind to the **possibilities** and opportunities that may now currently surround you in your world. In this money meditation, you must apply the *logic* of the millionaires mind technology software processes money accumulation gradation process. The **money** accumulation gradation process states that in order for you to make your first million, you first must learn to make a hundred thousand. And that in order for you to make your first hundred thousand, you first need to learn how to make some thousands. And to make some thousands, you need to scan your world and locate a hustle that can make you some **hundreds** consistently. So the first **short-term financial goal** that you set should be to find a way to hustle up some **hundreds** and thousands in order that you may raise your business start-up capital.

Your research should have determined the rough amount of money that you will need to raise in order to satisfy your business needs. The amount of money that you need to raise is the amount of money that you will need to focus on when setting your first **financial goal.** This **goal** should be incorporated into the **fabric** of the other goals that you set in your platinum plan. This first goal will serve as the basis for the development of all of your other bigger **goals** in the future. Take the time-out now to **meditate** and visualize in detail you achieving your goal of raising your start-up **money**. Imagine yourself hustling toward achieving this **goal by any legit** means necessary!

4. LOCATE A CASH SOURCE TO SUPPLY YOUR FINANCIAL NEEDS

Now for a second, let's zoom in and imagine that through your research, you have determined that you will need to raise **$50,000** to finance your business operation. Or maybe you have ascertained that you will need to *hustle up* **$125,000** to set your business up. Once your business financial needs are known, then you must begin the process of scanning your world to locate a cash source to supply your financial needs. Cash sources that you can capitalize upon will come in the form of beneficial people, places, or things. Your focus when scanning your world for valuable people, places, or things is to find a cash source in one of these forms that will sufficiently supply with you with a stream or streams of income to satisfy your needs. This **cash** source will allow you to accumulate the **money** that you need to achieve each of your financial goals. This cash source is your opportunity to adopt a hustle that will help you to get into the game. A hustle is any money-generating business activities that can serve as a legitimate means for raising the money to finance your business **operation.** Now let's zoom in and take a closer look at how to locate some people, places, or things that you can tap into and use as a hustle:

➡ People. Beneficial people are any of your **family, friends,** or associates with deep **pockets** that can open up some **doors** for you, or put you in the way of opportunity to begin hustling and making some money. Look for people who are connected and can help you get connected. The goal is to turn these people to your advantage by getting them interested in your ideas and plans.

Scan your world to look for people who can teach you how to make the money that you **need** to raise. You can begin by **looking** into your immediate family to find someone who might have a mind for making a dollar and that can put you on. If you do not have any family who can help you out, then you must look at your friends. Your friends can be found in your e-mail contacts, in your cell phone, or your **friends** in your social networks such as **Facebook** Instagram and LinkedIn or Twitter. Or maybe you have some **business associates** that can help you to get into the game. The goal is to find people who have money, people who know people with **money,** or people who know how to make some **money** in today's new economy. Connect with these types and make it happen! There may be some **beneficial** people in your life **right** now. Your job, then, is to find them!

➡ Places. Look into your life for places that you can go to help change the course of your financial destiny. If you live in a broken town where there is a slow flow of cash, then you might have to get up and go. Go to where the money and **opportunity** is flowing. The longer you stay stagnated in a broken town, the longer it will take to get your **dreams** off of the ground. Follow your **dreams** wherever they take you! America is a big place so if need be, move around! **Imagine** a city across America that has the **money flowing,** or the opportunity that you seek! Take your show on the road! Seek and you shall find!

➡ **Things.** If you can **locate a hot product** or service to **sell,** then establish a **solid supply** of what you are **selling** and then further establish **a solid group** of customers for what you are selling then you have found a beneficial **thing!**

5. UNLEASH YOUR HUSTLE!

"E pluribus unum." This was the original motto adopted by America, which means "Out of many, one." As a hustler on the rise, you must also adopt this as your own motto. You must remix the saying by adapting it to your situation. The remixed version will state, "Out of many hustles, one!" To get into the game, all you will need to find is one hustle that you can capitalize upon and use as your come up! Americans have been following their dreams of riches for years. Imagine the gold rush days when people across America would travel west to follow their dreams! Some people prospered and found their fortunes. Others failed. It's all in the game. You must follow your dreams.

Now once that you have located a solid cash supply to take advantage of, then the *next step* in the process is to unleash your hustle! As with everything in the millionaires **mind** technology software information, unleashing your hustle will follow a simple process. The process of unleashing your hustle:

1. Hustle.

2. Stack.

3. Save.

4. Reinvest to expand and grow.

Now let's zoom in to *examine* the process of unleashing your hustle! What does **unleashing your** hustle involve? **Unleashing your hustle** is where you begin striving in your life to accumulate the specific amounts of **money** that you will need in order to achieve each of the **goals** that you have set within your platinum **plan.** Recognize that if you are to rise to achieve the *new* American magazine dream, you must let your hustle loose! This is where you get off of the bench, get into the game, start **dribbling** the ball, and **score** some points to win! Only in the **money** game you will have to punch the clock and go to work to win. Day in and day, out you must walk through the world with your money consciousness and **business** mind turned on and turned up!

Next, we will switch lanes to observe what it means to stack. For a moment, imagine that your life has given you lemons. So in turn, you make the most out of your life by making **lemonade.** And then you set up **a lemonade stand** to make some **money.** As the money rolls in, you must get into the habit of *managing* the money that flows through your lemonade stand. Now say for instance that you have set a goal to sell a thousand dollars' worth of lemonade. As you make some money, you begin to let the money pile up until you have a thousand dollars stacked up. Stacking your money is the process of **guiding** each dollar that you make and using each dollar as a strategic tool to achieve each of your immediate financial goals that you have set.

Saving should be a no-brainer. Yet when most of us make some money, we usually skip this crucial step. The concept of saving or paying yourself first should always be applied to your hustle on the road ahead. Savings is the *key* to unlock your success.

Why? **Half** of **hustling** is all about making some money. While the other half of the game is all about keeping the money that you make. So understand that if you are to win, you must learn to save **money.** Learn to be *patient.* Why? Because **growing** your million-dollar nest egg will be a gradual process that takes *time* and *discipline.* So when hustling, you must train yourself to develop the habit of paying yourself first each time that you reach a milestone on the road to **making** some **money.** For example, let's say that you stack up a lump sum of cash. At that time, you then put away 10 to 20 percent of the **money** that you hustle up away toward growing your million-dollar **baby. Go savings!**

The final step in unleashing **your** hustle is to invest or reinvest a **portion** of the **money** that you have hustled up to keep **growing** your **dough** each step along the way up the money accumulation gradation ladder! So now that you know, let's go!

Chapter 8

Building Your First Business

Now let's get your brain in the business game! In this chapter, we will focus on building your first business in your profit portfolio! *Phase 3*. This first business will play a vital role in helping you to achieve each of the goals and objective strategies in your **platinum** plan. The focus of this first business you construct is to establish a solid stream of income through the process of investing the money that you have hustled up. Thus, you will be setting in **motion** the **money** accumulation gradation process toward building your million-dollar nest egg! With that in mind, I will suggest at this moment that you stop to sit back, **think,** reflect, and absorb all of the **information** that you have read in this book up until this point. Then after that, we will fast forward to presuppose that in time, you will have *successfully* hustled, stacked, and saved up your business start-up cash at which time you will be prepared to set up shop!

Now to begin moving forward with the business-**building** process, you will need to activate your business mind. Once your business mind is activated, then you will need *to turn* your attention to focus on *laying* a solid **foundation** to **build** your first business upon. Now ask yourself. What is the foundation upon which all successful businesses are built? In my judgment, all successful businesses are built upon the foundation of the forces of supply and demand. With that, the forces of supply and demand are the foundation upon which you must begin building your first business!

To better *understand* the concepts of **supply** and demand, *zoom* in to envisage that every year across America, millions of businesses are born. Then ask yourself. Each year out of all of these millions of businesses that are born, how many of them live on to survive, thrive, and grow to become a success? As you can imagine, not many of these businesses survive. Now ask why is this a fact? The answer in my opinion is that many of these businesses are built upon weak demand. The idea is that if the demand for what a business is offering for sale is strong, then the business stands a greater chance to succeed. And on the flip side, if the demand for what the business is offering for sale is weak, then so shall be the revenues for which the business stands to generate. With that, rewind your mind back to an earlier chapter where you were walked through the process of choosing a hot product or service to build your first business around. That product or service ought to be engineered to satisfy a strong desire, want, need, or problem in a large group of people. (Note—finding new products that can be introduced to large groups of people is a *key* element in building a winning business.)

For purposes of clarity in the *world* of business, demand is defined as the amount of a product or service that a specific number of people are ready and able to buy at a given time at a certain price. And **supply** is the amount of a product or service that a business is **willing** and able to produce and make available to the market at a particular time at a specific price. Now to see how these forces work, zoom out to look at America's consumer markets with an eye to see how the forces of supply and demand *influence* our lives as consumers. Specifically imagine all of the products and services that your *life* demands that you purchase each day to *satisfy* your needs.

As an individual consumer, each day your life may demand that you *purchase* products such as toothpaste, energy drinks, cigarettes, gas, and so on. And further your lifestyle may demand that you purchase services such as cell phone service, fine dining, Internet access, massages, or anything that you may pay money for each day. This is an aspect of supply and demand that we are all familiar with. Realize that each and every product or service that you go out and purchase each day is being supplied to you through someone else's business. Now going beyond **imagining** the satisfaction of your own personal needs, imagine all of the businesses across your city in the game that are supplying people with the stuff that they demand. Then zoom out to imagine all of the businesses that operate to supply people with products and services across your state. Then zoom out to **imagine** all of the hottest products and services that are in demand across America today. Then picture all of the people that are willing and able to buy these things. And then imagine all of the businesses that are able and willing to supply the people across America with all of these products that we all demand.

This is supply and demand at work. So with this concept in mind, before you jump into the business game, you first must strive *hard* to develop a *clear grasp* of the concepts of supply and demand and how they influence your life, your business, your target business industry, our economy as well as economies across the globe. And once that is done, you must then go further to test the strength of the demand for the product or service that you plan to build your first business around. And at that point, if you ascertain through your research that a strong **demand** *exist* for what you plan to offer for sale, then and only then should you begin **building** your first business!

So once again in the sphere of business, strong demand gives birth to *hot* products and services. And *hot* products and services are then developed in to fully functioning companies. At this point, we will assume that you have selected a *hot* product and service with a strong demand to **build** your first business around. Once the product or service selection process is complete, then you can begin the process of giving shape to your business. Giving shape to your business will entail that you first develop a detailed plan describing how it is that you will bring your business into existence. On paper, you will attempt to bring together the components of a fully functional business. And then you will describe the path that you will take for growth and profitability. The focus of your plan should be to describe the goals:

1. Produce your product or service.

2. Manage the money going in and out of your business.

3. Hire *star* people to work for your organization.

4. Market, promote, and advertise to attract customers to your business.

5. **Distribute** your product or service to your market.

These are five processes that you must learn and perfect in order to begin constructing a winning business in your **industry**. Generally, the **goal** is to bring these five component parts together in **balance** and **harmony** with your budget. It's all set in *motion* with you first gaining the knowledge of your product or service. *Next*, you will need to create a business with the input and output capacity to supply the demand.

Always remember, it takes money to make money! Ultimately, the first business that you make up your mind to build will be influenced a great deal by your budget, or the amount of money that you are able to hustle up through fund raising. Therefore, when you do actually reach the point that you are ready to set up shop, if at that time you believe that you will be not be able to raise the money to invest in the business you envisioned in the "Build Winning Business Blueprints" chapter, then do not be troubled. As an aspiring entrepreneur, there are several ways to make lemonade out of your life's lemons. There are choices you have to get your foot into the door:

THE ART OF MAKING MONEY

> 1. Give **birth** to a **brand**-new business.
>
> 2. Buy a business operation that is already in existence.
>
> 3. Buy into a franchise opportunity!

Each of the options described above has their pros and cons. Try imagining each opportunity as a potential vehicle that can possibly help you reach your destination. Again, which vehicle you choose will be determined by how much money that you have to spend. And beyond this, you will need to consider which business **opportunity** offers you the most feasible opening for acquiring a business that will allow you to **build** a solid customer base as rapidly as possible. Overall, your focus should be to choose a business opportunity that presents you with the most practicable means for acquiring a company that will allow you to attract and build a solid group of paying customers.

Whether you intend to build a brand-new business from scratch, buy an existing business, or buy into a franchise opportunity planning is an essential characteristic for **building** a successful business in any **industry.** Your **plan** is a tool that describes how you will take your idea out of your mind and into the market. Your plan should describe how you will take your idea from whatever stage it is in its development to become a profitable enterprise. Your plan is whatever you make it to be. It can be as simple or as intricate as you choose. Your business plan is essential because this is how you plan to hustle up the money to achieve the goals in your platinum plan. The business designs that you draw up shall give your platinum plan *traction.*

At this stage, you will begin the process of giving shape to your business on paper. Gather a quantity of paper, a new document screen on your computer, or something that you can record your *thoughts* on. Once you have your recording tools *on hand,* you then will need to find a place where you can focus and **think.** Once you are focused, take some time-out to reflect upon this. There is no one universal system used to develop a business plan. Generally, a *comprehensive* business plan should express:

> ➡ **Bring together** the **components** of a **fully functional business.**
>
> ➡ **Bring** your **business** into **existence.**
>
> ➡ **Attract paying customers** and **investors.**
>
> ➡ **Recoup** your **investment.** And **explain** how much of **a profit** that you stand to **gain.**
>
> ➡ **Build** your **business now** and in the **future.** (Your **business plan should describe** in **detail** the **path** your **company** will follow to **profitability** and **growth.**)

1. Introducing your product or service.

    ➡ *Demand summary.* Before you begin building any business in any industry, you must first determine through investigation if a true demand or market exist for what your business plans to offer for sale. Specifically, you must measure the demand and determine its strength. In other words, you must determine how many people in your city, state, or **country** are out there right now **willing** and able to buy your product or service and how *eager* they are to make a purchase. In this section of your plan, give a detailed explanation of the demand that you have uncovered.

- *Product or service description.* In this segment of the plan, you must describe your product or service. Describing what desire, want, need, or problem that your product or service will satisfy in the market. Give a narrative of what makes what you are offering **unique** and what sets it apart from your competitions product.

- *Competitions product or service description.* In this segment of the plan, describe the products or services that the competition is putting on the market for sale.

- Describe what desire, want, need, or problem that their product or service will satisfy in the market. Give a narrative of what makes what they are offering to the market unique and the threat that it *poses* to your businesses sales forecast.

- *Demand cycle.* Give a depiction of where your product is in the context of its product life **cycle.** Is your **industry new,** is it growing, is it **maturing,** or **declining?**

- *Demand forecast.* Here, you will *attempt* to calculate or measure how much demand exists in the *world* for your product or service. There are many methods available. You can use market research, customer feedback, or make an educated guess. Whichever method you *employ,* you must use the information you gather to make demand forecast predictions. In this section of your plan, you must guesstimate how much product you will need to produce to supply the demand.

- *Demand capacity.* After determining how much *actual* demand exists, you must go further to determine what measure of the demand that your company can realistically supply. Give a description of how much product you are able to produce with your budget and how **much** you are **willing** to produce.

➤ *Production design layout.* In this part, you will give a description of how your production facility will be designed. Describe the technology your company will use, the equipment, the location of the site, and anything else that you can think of that will go into the process of producing your product or service.

(Overall, this phase of your business plan should express the specific actions that you will take to bring together the factors of production to supply the demand. Here, you will describe the materials, component parts, or **things** needed to produce your product. Also give a description of your suppliers, what they are supplying you with, and any alternative suppliers you have on deck in case of an emergency. Explain the contract agreement that you have or plan to establish with your suppliers.)

2. Managing the money flowing in and out of your business.

   ➤ *Financial forecast.* Summarize your company's financial projections. This section will describe how you will invest your start-up cash. How long it will take to recoup your investment. And finally, project when your company will turn a profit. Describe how you will raise money to finance your operations from day of inception forward. Explain how money will be allocated. Illustrate your businesses financial needs, and how they will be satisfied present and future. For example, how much it will cost to finance producing your inventory for today and in the future.

3. Hiring star people to work in your organization

   ➤ *Star management team.* If needed, give a description of the process that you will employ to assess management needs.

How you will attract, hire, **train,** develop, compensate, and promote your *star* management team. Give a *narrative* of the education credentials, business experience, financial backgrounds, and any other special skills or talents that each candidate will bring to your organization.

➡ *Star staff team.* This *element* of your plan is where you asses and forecast your wide-ranging staffing needs. Determine how many people you will need to help operate your business. Explain the process that you will apply to attract, hire, train, develop, compensate, and promote your star employee team. Teamwork makes the dream work! Your staff can make or break your company so hire stars!

4. Marketing

➡ *Fundamental marketing environments.* Your business will not exist within a bubble. Marketing environments cover every environment that surrounds your business, your customers, your potential customers, and the broad consumer public. There are many major trends that develop within these influential environments. This part of your plan ought to describe the current and future trends that you see taking shape:

➡ The current local, state, national, and global economic environments.

➡ The current business environment surrounding your market today.

➡ The modern technological environment of your business industry.

➡ The culture of your target customer's **community.**

➡ The legal environment that regulates the industry in which you will compete.

➡ The city or forum in which your business will be born, live, and grow.

➡ And the current social, ethical, and political environment that surrounds you within your chosen **field** of business.

Scanning and studying each of these key environments should help you gain a greater perspective of the characteristics of your target market. To understand your market, you must thoroughly identify with their desires, wants, needs, and their problems. As stated before, you must get into their skin to see the world through their eyes. This process will allow you to create products or services your market adopts.

1. Promotion and **advertising** to attract customers to your business

   ➡ *I Promotional messages.* This part of your plan is where you explain your complete plan to establish a *two-way* dialogue between your business and its customers. You must describe how you will gain their attention, lure them in, and make the sale. The goal of your communications plan is to establish a long-lasting, loyal relationship with paying customers. The more you can relate to your audience, the better you can communicate messages to them that will potentially increase sales.

   ➡ *Advertising.* This is the section of your promotional plan where you describe your company's campaign to communicate your promotional messages to your target market audience. Here, you must describe the mediums that you will use to communicate through. These can include but are not limited to the Internet, television, radio, magazines, newspapers, direct mail, telephone, and mobile devices.

The goal of all advertisements your company produces is to generate sales.

➡ *Company concept.* This part of your plan should illustrate your business design. Briefly *illuminate* your vision of the present and future of your company, your market, and your industry. Give a brief history of your company. Explain how you will bring your business into existence. Give a succinct *narrative* of your business schooling, your business experience, your financial background, and any other special skills or talents that you bring to your organization.

➡ *Business goals.* In this section, you should list all of your company's financial goals as well as any other goals that you may have for your business. When *writing* this part of your plan, *keep in mind* that the purpose of your business is to generate profits! You must describe in detail when you anticipate your business will breakeven, recoup your investment, generate some positive cash flow, and make a solid profit. Explain how you will achieve each goal. Your goals should also flow together with the goals and strategic objectives within your platinum plan.

➡ *Budget forecast.* Every phase of your business plan will have a financial dimension. Here, you must put in writing a detailed accounting of your budget allocations describing how much money will be distributed to accomplish each phase of your plan. Your funds will be limited, so you must use what you got! How much money will be allocated for production, **marketing,** staffing, and so on?

2. Distributing your product or service to your market:

    ➡ *Distribution infrastructure.* Describe in detail the system that you will use to distribute your product or service to your market. You must fashion a **distribution** system for your business with the input and output capacity to supply the demand. Your distribution arrangement plan must put in plain words the specific places that your customers can go to make purchases. The points of contact where your customers can make a purchase with your company can take the form of a physical store location, or maybe on the Internet in the form of an online store.

Build your business identity.

- Choose a few possible names you can use. Then narrow down your choices to one. Perform a search to determine if the name can be legally used in the *real* world of business as well as in the *world* of cyberspace. Make your business name official.

- Apply for a patent if your business will put a new invention on the market.

- Choose the location of your *office* headquarters. This will house your command center. This is where you will launch your campaigns to corner your market.

- File the necessary papers with your *local* or *state* government to register your business as a sole proprietorship, partnership, or as a corporation.

- Purchase all of your business supplies, computers, and equipment.

- Install business phone lines, *hook up* Internet service, and get computer intranets and extranets up and **running.**

- Open up your business bank accounts.

- Look into and satisfy insurance needs for your business type.

- Apply for business EIN number if you will hire employees.

- Build up your inventory if you will offer a physical product for sale.

- Purchase your business cards, stationary, promotional materials, and things.

- Prepare for takeoff. Launch your business! Then open up the doors of your business to the public and let the games begin!

Take your time and get your business plan right. There's no right or wrong format to use. It's your plan. Do it your way! Now let's focus on your profit portfolio. Let's go!

Chapter 9

- Manage Your Profit Portfolio

So here we are! In this chapter, we will fast forward immediately to visualize that distant moment in the future where you have built a successful business and now have moved your life from point **A to point** money! Point **money** is the **point** where your plans with any luck will have bore fruit, and your business has begun to generate some profits. Now in business as in life, there are never any guarantees of success. With that said, we will *believe* that your business will become a success and that some time in your *future,* you will have money to blow! The question at that moment will be what do you do with your new**found** riches? In this situation, most people will be overjoyed and then be driven to go out and celebrate! This is a *fatal mistake* that can get your *wheels spinning* in the mud very quickly! Once your business has produced some profits at that time, you must resist the urge to go out and splurge at all cost!

That means no popping bottles, no partying, no shopping, and absolutely no *new* cars! Got it? Why is this important? As a business owner, you will learn that half of the battle will be to first recoup your investment and to make some profits. And once you make some money, the second half of the battle is to keep the money that you make. So *learning* and *applying* smart money management tactics will be a must on the road ahead. Now if you're good with money and know how to stack and save, then *great!* If not, you must learn fast to *effectively* manage **your profit portfolio!** *Phase 4.*

At this *moment,* let's *zoom* in to **picture** that future **moment** where your first business produces some *rock-solid* profits! Now you may choose to organize your business as a sole proprietorship, a partnership, or as a corporation. But regardless of how you choose to *organize* your business, in order for you to pay your bills, you will need to pull money out of your business as personal income. The money streams that you draw from your business over every twelve-month cycle should be the money you use in your profit portfolio. How you manage the income that you touch will be central to your success! So that brings us to the *next* big question! What is a profit portfolio? A profit portfolio is a ***profit*** picture made up of two component parts:

Component part no. 1. Business unit *DNA*. This element of your profit portfolio will give you a snapshot of a single business unit or a family of business units that you own and control. Each business should be *viewed* as a strategic investment vehicle that you exploit to establish a stream or streams of income. These income streams are tools to help you achieve each of the goals and objective strategies in your platinum plan.

Additionally, this component part should have an element built in that is designed to measure the performance of each business unit in your profit portfolio.

Component part no. 2. If *one management system*. This element of your profit portfolio will give you a snapshot of the money management system that you have got to establish in order to effectively **track,** manage, and direct your **profit distribution** flows. This management system ought to explain how the money that you pull out of your business will be distributed to accomplish each of your personal financial goals.

COMPONENT PART NO. 1. BUSINESS UNIT *DNA*

*Elements of a business **unit:*** Each business that you own and control in your profit portfolio is a unit. You may start small with just *one single* business unit, or you may be more ambitious and have a *vision* of **building up a multi-unit** business organization. The first business unit you erect then can become the parent company that spawns a family of companies that you establish in the future. Each unit is a component part of the whole. Each unit is formed around a product or a product family that is attached to a market. To be successful with each unit, you must establish an *enduring* business relationship with the product market's group of people. Each unit will be a stand-alone entity that can be severed from the whole business organization without disrupting the balance and flow of the other business units within the organization. Each entity will be equipped with its own asset foundation, be capable of generating its own cash flow, and have its own individual financing requirements. Further, each unit must be allowed the flexibility and freedom to grow.

Now as each unit begins to operate and generate revenues, it will further be required that you develop a system to periodically gauge the performance of each business unit and the strength of its profit streams. In this system, a performance ruler must be put in place. Now the first business unit you set up and its accounting systems will be unique. The same will go for the structure of your profit portfolio's *business performance ruler* you create. This system will help determine where your future growth efforts should be concentrated and identify which units should be liquidated.

THE ART OF MAKING MONEY

Profit Portfolio: Business Unit DNA

example

1. *Star product* and *service genetic material.* A product or service that is destined to be famous will *start* with a strong demand. It ought to be market driven, have mass appeal, and have the potential to give birth to a family of related products.

2. *Market structure configuration:* The focus with market structure design is to design products or services that can be introduced to large markets with *strong* DNA. A market with *strong* DNA is a large market that is configured to *grow* rapidly. And one that can support sustainable, rapid growth one can control.

3. *Barrier to entry.* Ideally, an attractive business industry to invest and set up an operation in will have a low barrier to entry. Many industries offer high profit margins as well as high barriers to enter. Scan business industries to *look* for business opportunities that offer high profit margins and low barriers to entry.

4. *Investment requirements.* Preferably, business opportunities to *seek* out will require a low to moderate investment sum. Further, a solid opportunity should allow one to breakeven and turn a healthy profit in optimal time. (Investment sums and returns on investments will *vary* from business to business.)

1. *Competition.* When faced with strong competition, seek to eliminate them, align with them, or neutralize their products effectiveness in the market.

2. M*arket share positioning.* The objective when entering a *new* market is to enter the market **first.** One enters the market first to gain a strong **market** position. If one can't enter the market first, then be the first company to establish the number two position. Why? Statistically, the companies that enter the market first and second usually gain the most dominant positions in terms of market share.

3. *Supply sources.* In order to survive and thrive in an industry, one must *identify* strong supply sources to tap into and connect with. One's companies input capacity will influence the balance and flow of the output capacity. Establish strong supply sources to flood the supply chain and distribution channels.

4. *Financial strength.* It takes money to make money! Sufficient capital is *necessary* to bankroll any operation from day one, or the plan will be dead in the water. So before setting up any business unit, first assess one's financial strength. One's financial strength is the ability to adequately finance an operation from point A to point money! Establish strong financing to operate and grow the operation!

5. *Business goals* and *objective strategies.* Typically, smart and successful business people are skilled in *the art of* setting realistic, practical goals and objective strategies for their businesses. Learning and applying this skill is a must!

6. Planning. Entrepreneurial *business leaders* somehow or other gain the knowledge of continuous *strategic* business **planning. Planning** is an *essential* **skill** you have got to adopt! Every business unit must have a solid plan behind it to succeed!

7. *Marketing arm.* The marketing arm of each business unit should *seek to fully* exploit all of the long-established, universal, modern-day marketing practices. While at the same time employing *bold* guerilla marketing tactics that the company develops or adapts to *relentlessly* pull in business and generate profits.

8. *Production facility.* Build a state-of-the-art production facility that applies the most cutting-edge technology within the industry to produce the products for a company. The goal of the production facility ought to be to *achieve* economy of scale. Further, when choosing a *location,* savvy *entrepreneurs* find locations that offer the most strategic logistical positions to distribute products to a market.

9. *Star* teams. *Star* teams ought to be *assembled* in production, marketing, accounting, staffing, and all spheres of the business to win! A strong team should be made up of highly trained, book-smart, street-smart, shrewd, money-conscious, business-minded, talented, and productive *star* individuals who are team players.

10. *High performance accounting system.* A *professional* accounting system ought to produce monthly income statements, balance sheets, and cash flow statements that all leaders in the business can study and use to make *real* time decisions.

COMPONENT PART NO. 1. BUSINESS UNIT *DNA. (continued)*

Profit portfolio business performance ruler. Companies across America in the business arena frequently use a tool called benchmarking to set performance standards for their businesses. The purpose of benchmarking is to assist a company in *achieving* superior performance and a competitive advantage in the market. When fashioning a business performance ruler system within a profit portfolio, I would suggest that the benchmarking concept be used as a guide. Now keep in mind that each unit that you set up and its accounting systems will be unique. And the same will go for the structure of the *business performance rulers* you create to measure the performance of each unit.

In general, a performance gauging system will involve:

1. Identifying all of the processes that a company applies in production, marketing, staffing, accounting, and all other spheres of the business that may need improvement. This identification process will help to determine the company's *in-house* strengths and weaknesses. The results of this will provide a baseline to compare a company's performance with others in the *selected* business industry.

2. Do research to determine who the leading companies are in the **industry.** Compare the company's in-house processes with those of the leading companies in the business industry. This comparison will allow one to fashion a performance ruler to measure the results of the comparative analysis to make improvements.

3. Implement *changes* in each unit to increase the strength of each profit stream.

At the point that the profits within a portfolio start to grow, a system must be built in the performance ruler system to perform a *more in-depth* portfolio analysis. This aspect of the system must establish a method for looking into each company to take a look at each of its individual products and product families. This is done to detect the strongest and weakest profit earners. Each product or product family should be *viewed* as streams of **income.** The **focus** here is to develop a **methodology** for **spotting** units that are pulling in the money and may deserve more investment dollars. Based on the results of the evaluation, it then must be decided which products to invest more money in building up. And on the flip side, the system must spot which units that are not performing well and maybe should be liquidated. To assist in this process, developing a system for each unit to warehouse and mine its *data flows* to discover meaningful patterns or trends that takes form within each unit is a prudent decision. Why? The patterns or trends you discover can guide in the decision making process of deciding which unit products or product families should *ultimately* stay or go!

The overall idea is that each business unit you **build** is to be viewed a strategic investment vehicle that you can exploit to establish streams of income. These income streams are tools to help you to achieve each of the goals and objective strategies in your platinum plan. So with component part 1 of a **profit** portfolio, the goal is to establish a system that will allow for one to find out how much money each unit is generating in profits. And then to use this data to decide how much cash will be pulled out of the business in the form of personal income. This money then must be tracked, managed, and directed to move you up the money accumulation gradation ladder!

COMPONENT PART **NO. 2.** *MONEY MANAGEMENT SYSTEM.*

As a business unit begins to generate some positive cash flow, this money in turn will begin to flow into your personal bank accounts. At this point, you must *fashion* a system to track, manage, and direct your personal finances to achieve the financial goals within your platinum plan and your life overall. The following guidelines will help to set in motion a money management system for keeping track of your profits:

➡ Step no. 1: Separate your personal and business finances. Establish and maintain separate bank accounts and credit lines for your personal and business finances.

➡ Step no. 2: Begin documenting every dollar you touch from the first time that you *pull* money out of the business on. That means keep accurate, detailed records of every transaction that you make. Make sure to maintain a separate record of accounting for your personal cash apart from your businesses finances.

➡ Step no. 3: Set up a record-keeping system to *store* all receipts and hard copies of your **financial** records. Keep all check stubs, cash receipts from purchases, and credit card statements. To be safe keep a duplicate set of records as a backup.

After you set up your money-**tracking** system, you must **fashion a budget plan** to manage and direct your profit distribution flows. This will assist you in achieving all of the personal financial goals that you set. The profit portfolio budget plan that you create will be fundamental to making your platinum plan a success!

Profit Portfolio: Money Management System Prototype

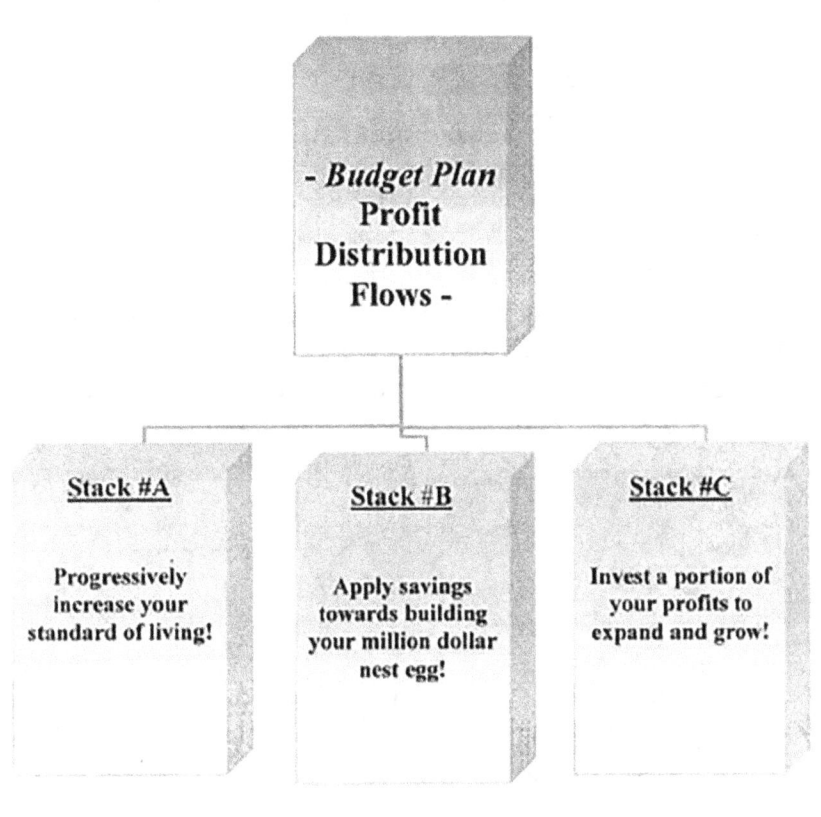

Now to begin the process of creating a budget plan that details the profit distribution flow *system* principle, picture this. You have hustled up some profits *through* your business. Yu generate some income through these profits. And now you have a *lump* sum of cash in hand. What do you do with the money? Now at that *time* if you have *bad* money-management skills, this is where your old reckless habits will show their face.

And this is when you will need to once again go into **boss mode.** In *boss mode,* your thinking should *begin to* **shift** where that single **stack** of **money** becomes, let's say, three stacks. That is stack A, stack B, and stack C. Each stack here represents a different financial goal in your *life* that you have set. For instance, when you receive a lump sum of dough, the system in place will *cause* the money in hand to be distributed to flow:

1. Stack A. In this illustration, stack A represents a financial goal that is set to progressively increase one's standard of living!

2. Stack B. In this illustration, stack B represents a financial goal that is set to **apply** savings toward **building the million-dollar** nest egg!

3. Stack *C.* In this illustration, stack C represents a financial goal that is set to invest a portion of the profits to expand and grow the profits in the portfolio!

There is no *right* or *wrong* way to distribute the profits that you touch. Use the example here as a guide to develop your *own* flow. Let's *zoom* in to take a closer look!

Budget Plan Profit Distribution Flows

Think forward to see this. Every year after the first day that you open up your business, you will need to perform certain task perfectly. Namely each year, you will *need* to *pay* yourself a **monthly** *wage* over and over, which will accumulate to become your yearly income. With your business, you may choose to create a payment structure where you *pay yourself weekly,* bi-weekly, **monthly,** or whatever you *choose*. As you *pull* this money out of your business as income, you must put a system in place to help you to *guide,* and *direct* your cash flow each time that you *touch* some cash each month. Over each year, *keep in mind* that *every dollar* that you touch will *move* you a step closer to your million-dollar goal. And that every green *dollar* that flows *through your hands* that is spent aimlessly will move you a step further away from your dreams.

Now **making your first** million will be the **primary** goal that you set within your **platinum** plan. And to achieve this big target **goal** of your **platinum plan,** you will be *required* to create a series of smaller business plans, which will be formed around smaller financial goals to help you reach your million-dollar goal step by step. So the amount of income that you draw from your business through your yearly salary will directly influence the immediate financial goals that you plan to achieve. It will then become *vital* that you first forecast and then settle upon how much of a *salary* you will draw each month over a twelve-month cycle. The sum that you are allocated each month will become the focal point of your annual budget plan distribution flows.

Each year, you will be required to form some *new* short-term goals around your monthly income. When **setting** these goals, the platinum planning goal-setting process should be used as a guide. That is set a *new* optimistic, pessimistic, and a realistic set of goals. Further, the cash flow **model** *set forth* will also serve as an example*:*

> ➡ Goal no. 1. Set a financial goal each month of the year that automatically causes a percentage of your income to be put forth *toward* you progressively increasing your standard of living! This cash will flow to *build* stack A.
>
> ➡ Goal no. 2. Set a goal to establish a stream of cash to flow automatically to *build* stack B. Stack B would represent a financial goal that you set *annually* to apply a percentage of your income to savings *toward* building your million-dollar nest egg! Let's go savings!
>
> ➡ Goal 3. Set a **monthly** goal to establish a stream of cash that will automatically flow to build stack C. Stack C *represents* a monthly financial goal that you would set to *invest* a percentage of the annual income to expand and grow the profits in your profit portfolio.

The focus here with each of the financial goals that you form and set is to begin devising a plan to manage and direct your personal cash flow. As stated, the first half of the game is *making* some money! And the second half is to keep as much of the money that you make through the process of applying smart money-management skills!

As you *create* streams of income, you must watch to see *where* your money is being spent, *how* it is being spent, and on what. Overall, the focus of creating a *yearly* budget plan is to start directing the cash that flows in and out of your hands to begin maximizing the power of each dollar. The **distribution** flow structure you create will also help you to achieve each goal component of your annual budget plan. Now the first goal component of your plan must establish how you plan to distribute a percentage of your income dollars to progressively raise your standard of living each year. While at the same time, you must set a goal component of your budget plan to apply a *percentage* of your income dollars to establishing and growing your million-dollar nest egg. This is a **big** deal. Why? You must set some **annual** savings goals and develop a goal component within your budget to achieve these goals each year. Why? It is your savings goal component that will illustrate how your cash will flow to grow your nest egg savings until it hatches to grow to be the million-dollar life of your dreams!

And lastly, you must learn the art of *reinvesting* the profits that you touch to expand and grow your personal net worth. So to begin *formulating* your annual budget plan distribution flows, you will need to perform some research. Your research should *seek* to *ascertain* and forecast how *much it will cost* you to satisfy your daily, weekly, and **monthly** needs over the span of the next year. Then you must forecast how much monthly income you will need to draw from your business to *cover* your overhead cost of living. With these figures, you must set your yearly financial goals. And then fashion a detailed budget plan describing how your cash flow will be distributed each month. When that is done, we will *zoom* in to evolve your *platinum plan*. Let's go!

Chapter 10

Evolve Your *Platinum Plan*

Focus! You see a vision of you *reaching* millionaire status! And further, you have *developed* a *platinum plan fashioned* around you building businesses that can move your life from point A to point money! Now once again before moving forward, let me state that there is no guarantee that you will *make* any money through your business, or that your **platinum plan** will be a success. Your success will *rest upon* the *strength* of your talents, your skills, your resources, your connections, and so on. But here, to *reinforce* positive thinking, we will assume that you will make a profit. And once you set your **platinum plan** *in motion* and your **business** begins to generate some positive cash flow, at that time, you will need to evolve your *platinum plan*. Phase 5. Evolving your *platinum* plan will involve that every yearly cycle, your business activities bear fruit that you take some time-out to check the status of your plan.

You must analyze your plan *annually* to determine how much money you have accumulated that year. And to see how far ahead you have advanced toward achieving your million-dollar goal. This is the *phase* where the optimistic and pessimistic goals that you have set the previous year will become more realistic. This new clearer view of reality coming into focus will help you to reorganize your efforts and recalibrate your goals. At this juncture everything will come down to your bottom line. Your bottom line is the overall profitability and success of your **platinum** plan *execution*.

Now *zoom* in to picture this. You are *sitting* at your desk in your office headquarters. While reclining in your big chair, you *stare* out over the skyline of your city. Through the window of your future you look ahead to envision what life will offer you *next*. After moments of contemplation and deep *reflection,* you pick up your platinum plan. Your platinum plan has been living for a year now. You study your plan to consider how successful you were at accumulating some profits this last year. Looking back, you also look at how effective you were at setting and reaching each of your short-term goals and objective strategies for the year. Further, you ask yourself questions:

> ➡ Where did I see myself this time last year when I looked ahead and set my goals?
>
> ➡ How successful was I at achieving my goals in my **platinum** plan this year?
>
> ➡ How successful was I at achieving my money accumulation goals this year?
>
> ➡ How successful was I at achieving my goals to stack some money up this year?
>
> ➡ How victorious was I at attaining my goals to save a percentage of my income toward **building** my **million**-dollar nest egg this previous year?
>
> ➡ How successful was I at achieving my goals to expand and grow this year?
>
> ➡ What did I do right this year with my **platinum** plan?
>
> ➡ What did I do wrong?
>
> ➡ What can I do to improve this next year?

Ask yourself questions like these to evolve your ***platinum*** *plan.* The answers that you *gain* from these questions will help to *open up a* *door* within your mind to *allow* you to begin perceiving new ways to grow your profits for the next year.

So how does a platinum plan evolve? Platinum plan evolution is the *natural organic process of annual business* development, growth, expansion, and change in the direction of your success! Thus each year, your platinum plan bears some fruit. At that time, your platinum plan should *automatically* evolve and change in an upward direction that follows the *logical* order of the money accumulation gradation ladder to success in your life! If you *recall* the money accumulation gradation logic *states* that in **order** to make your first **million** that you first must *find* ways to make some **hundreds!** And further up the ladder, you will need *to find ways* to make some thousands! And further to climb the ladder a *little higher*, you must locate ways to make some hundreds of thousands! And that everything in the process is *set in motion* with the force of your hustle and *through* the generation of money-making business ideas! Again, hustle is to strive energetically each day from sun *up until sun down* to achieve each of the goals you set in your master *hustle* plan! Specifically, *each day* of the *year forward*, you must hustle *hot* products through your businesses to pull in some profits!

And further each yearly cycle, you must continuously invest a portion of the profits your businesses accumulates to grow *bigger!* Now as you build up *stronger* profit streams every year, know that at the same time, you will be maneuvering yourself into a stronger position to do business from! This is called leverage. The more *leverage* you gain, the more money that you can accumulate to grow! *Remember* that each green dollar that you hustle up through *your* businesses will move you a step closer to achieving your dreams! While every dollar that you *squander* and spend on worthless pleasures will move you a step closer to the *poor* house. So let's get down to business!

So it should be clear to see the vital role that each business that you invest in each year and the profits that it **bears** will **play** in the **evolution** of your platinum **plan. Applying** the evolutionary process will help you move up to the next level on the money accumulation gradation ladder each year! *Visualize* and *remember* every year through this process that at that **point** in time your **business** investments bear **fruit,** you will be moving a little *closer* on and up the money accumulation gradation ladder *toward* reaching your million-dollar goal! So yearly at your businesses profit **juncture,** you advance along *toward* reaching a *new* financial goal you have set. You will be *required* to automatically evolve your ***platinum plan*** and your business plans simultaneously. That is your platinum plan and all of the sub-business plans that you create now and into the future every *twelve months* must evolve together harmoniously as a *unified* whole. Together, your plans must *constantly* develop, grow, expand, and change to *adapt* to any new *set* of circumstances that takes shape in your life.

Taken as a whole, the platinum plan evolutionary process is *designed* to help you keep your plans fresh and new so that your profit streams can grow stronger each year! So from here forward, psychologically you must train *your* brain to start *creating financial plans* and to *automatically* check the status of your platinum plan *at least once a year.* And also, you must **form** the **habit** of immediately *taking the necessary actions to* execute those plans. And then *ever so often measure* the *progress* of those plans in order to reorganize your efforts and recalibrate the *new* financial goals you set for each year. Overall, *developing* this practice will help you make better business *decisions* and help you to improve your **company's** bottom line.

All decisions that you make each year to develop, grow, expand, or change the direction of your business activities have got to be made *considering* the *reality* of the overall profitability of your company. So let's *zoom* in once again where you are **reclining** in your **big chair** in your office headquarters. At that moment, your thoughts are focused on masterminding your next big *money* and power moves for the next year. After that, you pick up your business plan and the yearly financial statements your company has *produced* for that *year.* You *start* in on studying your annual income and cash flow streams to see how effectively you have achieved your businesses financial goals that year. You study your company's revenues, its expenses, and its net income. Then you focus again on cash flow to determine how much money is available in your business bank accounts to invest in new ways to grow your business. Next, you zoom in to perform *some* research to learn how your customers, competition, technology, business environments, America, and the world as a whole have evolved this last year. You re-evaluate your business plans in *light* of these new changes that have *arrived*.

You **think** of ways that you can translate these *new* evolutionary changes you *notice* into *next year's* profits! Then later, you shift gears and bring *together* your company's teams to brainstorm and uncover more *ways* to grow your business. The purpose of your company's brainstorming *sessions* is to bring into play the collective intelligence of each team. Specifically, with each *meeting* as boss, you will seek to utilize the *collective* brains, talents, skills, and creativity of each team to generate and dream up *fresh* ideas and plans to retain your company's existing customers. And *to formulate* a twelve-month growth **plan** to attract **a *new* bigger** crowd of **paying** customers!

With a fresh perspective, you and your team scan and study the influential environments in which your business competes to look for *new* opportunities to increase sales! Particularly, you and your team *zoom* in to focus on studying and discussing the *effectiveness* of your company's *current* marketing strategies. Let's envision that this year, your company's marketing strategy has helped you pull in some big profits! So as a result, you *increase* your marketing budget. Using your marketing arm as a tool to increase your company's sales, you must be sure that your marketing, advertising, and *overall* promotions people are locating the most effective channels to communicate your marketing messages to your market audience. *Reach* and frequency of your *marketing messages is the key to* **attracting** *new larger groups of paying customers each year!* Along those lines, you begin to fashion your *new* growth plans for the next upcoming year. You and your team also brainstorm:

THE ART OF MAKING MONEY

1. Increasing your sales this approaching year through *introducing* new products or services to your existing customer base!

2. Introducing your current product or service to *new* target groups of people.

3. Increasing the volume of each transaction with your new or existing customers!

4. Completing multiple transactions with your company's new or existing customers!

5. Studying your businesses processes to lower the cost of producing your product!

6. Harnessing the power of any new technology that has been introduced and that is *currently* transforming the way that business is being done in your industry.

7. Locating new environments on the Internet and in the real world to sow the seeds of the promise of satisfaction in the minds of new potential customers!

ISHMAIL HAMED

Platinum Plan: Business Investment Annual Growth Planning

example

The process of investing your businesses profits each year to expand and grow your **platinum plan** investment holdings should be viewed **similarly** to farming. In this **illustration,** the process of investment farming is the process of **planting financial** seeds in the soil of demand that are raised, grow over time, and then are harvested each year in the *appropriate* season. Tax season is business harvest time each year. As soon as you invest any money in a business opportunity, at that *instant,* you are *setting* the business growth process in *motion.* Understanding this farming process, you must learn to be patient. Why? Just as you can't expect to plant a seed of corn in the ground and then tomorrow magically have grown fields of corn as far as the eye can see, you can't expect to invest money in a business opportunity and magically grow a business that *blossoms* into a money-making machine! So when you first invest in a business opportunity, be aware that the *start-up* phase will usually run a three-year *cycle.*

Also, when looking forward to *turning* a profit, you should *plan* to *turn* a profit within this first two- to three-year business start-up cycle. With this in mind, you will have to *fashion a growth plan* to invest a percentage of your yearly profits to grow your *businesses investments* the year after your first business becomes profitable! Understand the process of **planting,** growing, and harvesting crops year after year goes on and on. And the same goes for the process of growing your business investments each year!

Gaining a *realistic* perspective of business growth *cycles* will *enable* you to shape more realistic expectations in your **mind** of the time **frame** in which you can forecast a *return* on your investments. So as you focus on fashioning annual growth plans for a business in your platinum plan, *rewind* your *mind* back to *remember* that the *initial* seed-planting *stage* is always the most important *step*. Why? All business profits will *grow* from the product. So when you invest in any business opportunity, only expect to reap profits in the amounts *directly* related to the profit-pulling power of the product your company plans to produce. So from the *outset,* if the focus with a business you invest in is growth, then the aim of the business plans that you *devise* should be to sow the investment seeds in the soil of fertile demand that from the soil of fertile demand *grows* products with mass appeal! Products with mass appeal can be introduced to large markets! It is **large** groups of people who are **willing** and able to purchase your products that will *offer* you fields of fertile soil to grow your business!

So the more a product that a company is offering appeals to a large market, then the bigger the group of customers that the business can potentially **attract.** And without a product with the **pulling** power to attract **a big group** of **paying** customers, then you will have no business! So the focus of growth **planning** each approaching *year* is to grow profits through attracting bigger groups of paying customers! So after demand strength when *creating* a company's *upcoming growth* plans, you must focus on the product market's structural design. Why? At the outset, when engineering a product, it should be a product that can potentially grow into a market that can support sustainable, rapid growth. Your plans must *seek* to *harness* this growth potential!

As you **zone** in to construct a growth **plan,** you must gather your **platinum** plan and any relevant business plans first. Then through the ten-step planning *process,* you must follow these steps.

1. **Think** forward. Then **put** in writing a *succinct* description of the vision of growth that you have for your company for the next approaching year.

2. Perform some research such as mining your company's data. Then study your bottom line. Look at your company's net income. And then look at your company's available cash balance for the present moment.

3. Gather your facts and consider your options.

4. Decide upon which course of action that you will take to grow your profits!

5. Set your company's financial goals for the next upcoming year.

6. Clarify your objective strategies to coincide with your financial goals.

7. Create a twelve-month growth calendar. The twelve-month growth calendar must arrange into days, weeks, and months the activities and events that will unfold the upcoming *year* to *stimulate* forecasted growth.

8. Execute the growth plan.

9. Next, monitor your *annual* evolutionary and growth plans.

10. And then adjust and set your sites on the next year's evolution and growth.

Okay! So here you have reached the closing *chapter* of the *millionaires* mind technology software business-building *process!* Through this *process,* you have been *offered* a complete model of business building that you can duplicate for your *rise* in the American business arena! Congratulations!

Now before we end, let's *zoom* in to *take a closer look* at your life! At this *moment,* ask yourself this question. Where will your life take you financially from this point forward if you continue to follow the course that your life is set on at this present moment?

And then ask yourself. Where can your life *potentially go* financially if you follow the *path* that having *created* a platinum plan for *yourself have now* opened up? Just think. Everyone wishes for riches to come into their lives at one time or another. Yet the reality is that very few *people* will actually do something about it. Today you have big dreams! And perhaps *currently,* you, too, are *wishing* for *riches* to come into your life! Possibly you *wish* that *your life* will provide you with an **opportunity** to change your financial destiny. The platinum plan you have created is your window of opportunity that has now *opened up* through which you can *possibly* change your financial destiny! Through the door of your platinum plan a new **brighter** future is now in your **reach!**

So recognize that once you get active and take the model that I have laid out *within* the pages of this book, from out of this book, and put it into your life! That at that time, your magazine dreams will come alive! And then after the day your magazine dreams are born, then you must begin to hustle and strive each day forward to begin doing everything in your power to set your magazine dreams on a course where they become an inevitable reality! And with no time to waste, your single-*minded* focus must be to become a self-made person of money! And to rise to live your own tailor-made *version* of the new American magazine dream! So when you put this book down, begin working as hard as you *possibly* can to get your finances in order. And then once your finances are on track, *get moving* full speed ahead! With no turning back!

Now there is only so much that you can learn from a book! Yet at the same time, we need to read and **study** to *help* **build** up our brainpower. The information that I have introduced to you here through the pages of this ***millionaires*** mind technology book can be extremely useful in helping you to unlock the power that is buried within your mind. That is if you let it fully program your mind for success! When you are done reading this book, then I would *suggest* that you read this book again! And then read this book again! Study this book. Reflect upon each line in this book. Commit every word to memory if you can. And then once you are done reading and studying this book, then read in between the lines to gain a new perspective! And then when that's done, understand that the knowledge *contained* in this book is only a launching **pad** to get your **platinum plan** and **magazine** dreams off the ground! And after that the rest will be all up to you! With that said, I will leave you to ponder these thoughts.

Wherever you are today in your life money-wise, know that there is money and opportunity surrounding you today across America! To *turn* your financial condition around, you must begin looking at your *world* through the new eyes of your money consciousness and business mind to begin *perceiving* the business opportunities that are out there waiting for you! And then *start* **thinking** big! And dreaming bigger! And as you dream big, *remember* that America is the land where big dreams do come true and where insane fortunes are made! That in America, it doesn't matter if you have a *limited education* or *limited resources,* you can make it if you have the courage to try!

The question now is will you continue to *sit* on the *side lines* and *watch* life *pass* you by? Or will you suit up, **punch** the clock, and go to work stepping into the role of the boss?

Platinum Plan Execution: 3 Golden Rules!

Lastly, commit this to memory. The most intricate million-dollar plans that you *can* dream up in this *world* will be worthless if you don't take the first step! So understand that your *platinum* plan will only *come alive* through execution! So as you press forward *toward* platinum plan execution, follow the three *golden rules:*

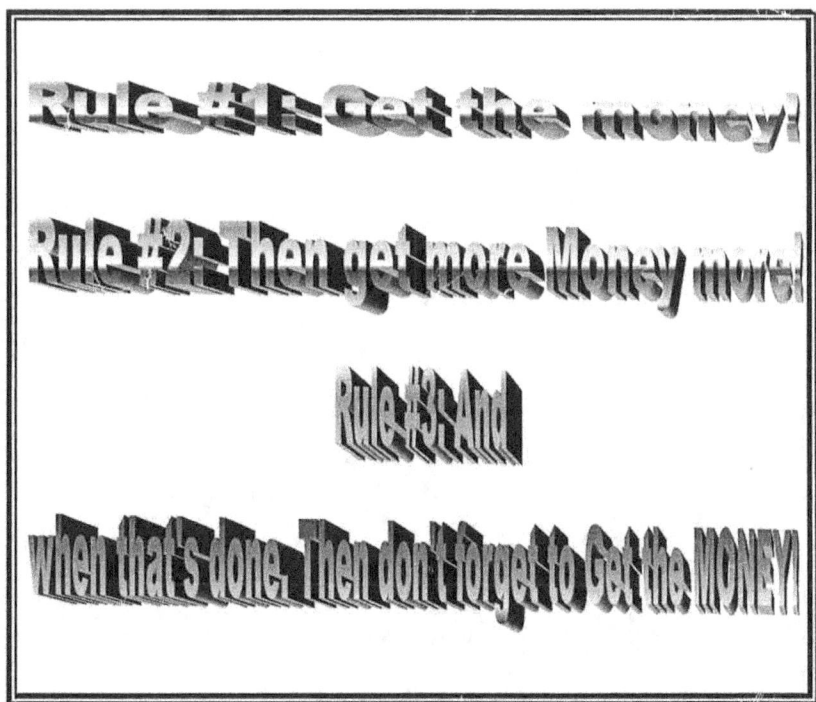

Rule #1: Get the money!

Rule #2: Then get more Money more!

Rule #3: And when that's done, Then don't forget to Get the MONEY!

Afterword

I wrote *The Art of Making Money* out of a sincere desire to help people in America and across the world achieve their dreams of accumulating money in large amounts! I wanted to write the most comprehensive book available today on the market. In writing this book, I have offered you everything that I believe that you will need to get started on your journey to the top! But remember that learning is a life-long process, not an end. So use the knowledge contained within the pages of this book as a foundation of knowledge that you build upon. As my knowledge of the subject matter *increases,* this book will be updated appropriately. I would love to hear from you to help improve future editions of this book!

Feel free to share your success stories with me. Tell me which chapters were specifically helpful to you and offer any suggestions for improvements. Also, let me know what may have caused you any confusion. Although I cannot guarantee you success in any form, the information contained in the pages of this book is based upon tried and proven principles of success! They work for those who work them! Before I go, I would like to extend this warning to you. Be very careful because if you follow the **guidelines** set forth in this **book,** you could very well make your first million! Best of luck, **my friend!** God bless the child who's got his own! Ready. Set. Let's go!

ISHMAIL

Notes

About the Author

This book has been written with hopes that it will provide you with the vision, motivation, and knowledge that you will need to potentially make your first million dollars! The author, Ishmail Hamed, wrote this book based upon his own life's experiences as well as input and insights from business associates whom have owned their own businesses and other entrepreneurs that Ishmail has interviewed, consulted, or conducted actual business with. Ishmail is a self-proclaimed business guru who has acquired extensive business knowledge through study, valuable lessons learned from real life experiences, and doing business. Ishmail comes from a long line of business owners who have owned and ran a variety of successful business enterprises. So it is safe to say that entrepreneurship is in Ishmail's DNA!

Specifically, Ishmail has acquired business mentoring from his father, Nazzim A. Hamed, his uncle Jerome McCoy, his cousin Walter Alexander as well as other family members and business associates who have imparted some essential business wisdom that has helped shape Ishmail's unique business perspective. Further, Ishmail gained hands on business training and experience through the process of running a marketing company for a family friend, the late John T. Hickey a.k.a. Jack. Jack and his business provided Ishmail with additional business mentoring in the realms of marketing and management. This hands-on experience managing Jack's company greatly helped mold and shape Ishmail's business outlook. Overall, Ishmail is a student of life, a player in the American money game, an entrepreneur, and a published author.

www.ingramcontent.com/pod-product-compliance
Lightning Source LLC
Chambersburg PA
CBHW070637220526
45466CB00001B/207